C·A·X·T·O·N

The Description
—of Britain—

C·A·X·T·O·N

The Description
—of Britain—

A MODERN RENDERING BY
MARIE COLLINS

PICTURE RESEARCH BY DEBORAH POWNALL

SIDGWICK & JACKSON
LONDON

To my parents, Alice and André Riffard, with gratitude

First published by Sidgwick & Jackson Limited
in Great Britain in 1988

First Paperback Edition October 1989

Copyright © 1988 by Marie Collins

ISBN 0-283-99754-0

Printed in Hong Kong
for Sidgwick & Jackson Limited
1 Tavistock Chambers, Bloomsbury Way
London WC1A 2SG

CONTENTS

A SELECTIVE CHRONOLOGY OF MAJOR EVENTS IN
THE DESCRIPTION OF BRITAIN

[with approximate relative dates, many of them taken from Geoffrey of Monmouth's *History of the Kings of Britain*]

WORLD	BRITAIN	MISCELLANEOUS
c. 1240 BC The destruction of Troy by the Greeks Aeneas escapes to Italy to found a kingdom	Aeneas's great-grandson Brutus leads the subjugated Trojans from Greece to Britain and rules as first king	
c. 1075–1035 BC [Samuel is a judge in Israel]	Queen Gwendolen, who had Habren put to death, rules	
c. 1011–971 BC [King David reigns in Judea]	Ebrancus rules	
c. 971–931 BC [King Solomon rules]	Leil rules	
c. 874 BC onwards [The prophet Elijah]	Rudhudibras and Bladud rule	
753 BC Traditional date of the founding of Rome	Leir ('King Lear') rules	
Before 701 BC	Moliuncius rules	
Before 390 BC	Lud rules	
55–54 BC	Julius Caesar invades Britain	70–19 BC: Virgil, Roman poet and author of *The Aeneid*
8–7 BC [Birth of Christ] AD 43	The Emperor Claudius comes to Britain Arviragus rules	
AD 208–211	The Emperor Severus comes to Britain and refurbishes Hadrian's Wall	
AD 306–337 Constantine the Great rules as Emperor		AD 354–430: Lifetime of St Augustine of Hippo, author of *The City of God* and *The Confessions*
AD 450–455	Germanic invaders, led by Hengist, come to Britain Vortigern rules	
AD 520–542 approx.	'King Arthur' rules	
AD 560–616 approx.	Ethelbert rules in Kent	
AD 597	St Augustine, sent by Pope Gregory, comes to Kent to convert Britain	
		c. AD 600: Isidore becomes Bishop of Seville *c.* AD 625: Paulinus becomes Bishop of York

WORLD	BRITAIN	MISCELLANEOUS
AD 635	Aidan brings Celtic Christianity to northern Britain and settles on Lindisfarne	AD 633–641: (St) Oswald rules in Northumbria AD 664: St Chad becomes Bishop of York. St Cuthbert becomes Prior of Lindisfarne and dies 687
AD 669	The Greek Archbishop Theodore arrives in Canterbury	
AD 735	Death of the Venerable Bede	AD 731: Bede completes his *Ecclesiastical History*, one of the ultimate sources of *The Description of Britain*
AD 757–796	Offa rules in Mercia	
AD 793	Viking raids begin	
AD 800 Charlemagne, king of the Franks, is crowned Emperor in Rome		
AD 869–870	The Danes overrun East Anglia and kill King (St) Edmund	
AD 871–899	Reign of King Alfred the Great	Alfred's laws and translations
AD 886 approx.	The boundaries of the Danelaw are agreed between Alfred and the Dane Guthrum	
AD 959–975	Reign of King Edgar	
AD 978–979	Murder of King Edward ('the Martyr')	
AD 1016–1042	Reign of the Dane Canute and his sons	
AD 1042–1066	Reign of King Edward the Confessor	
AD 1066–1087	Reign of King William I ('the Conqueror')	
AD 1087–1100	Reign of King William Rufus	
AD 1100–1135	Reign of King Henry I	1120s: Writings of the historian William of Malmesbury
AD 1135–1154	Reign of King Stephen	1100–1135: Flemish settlement in Wales
		1138: Geoffrey of Monmouth's *History of the Kings of Britain*
AD 1154–1189	Reign of King Henry II	
AD 1189–1199	Reign of King Richard I ('the Lionheart')	Later 12c: the writings of Gerald of Wales
AD 1170	Murder of St Thomas Becket	

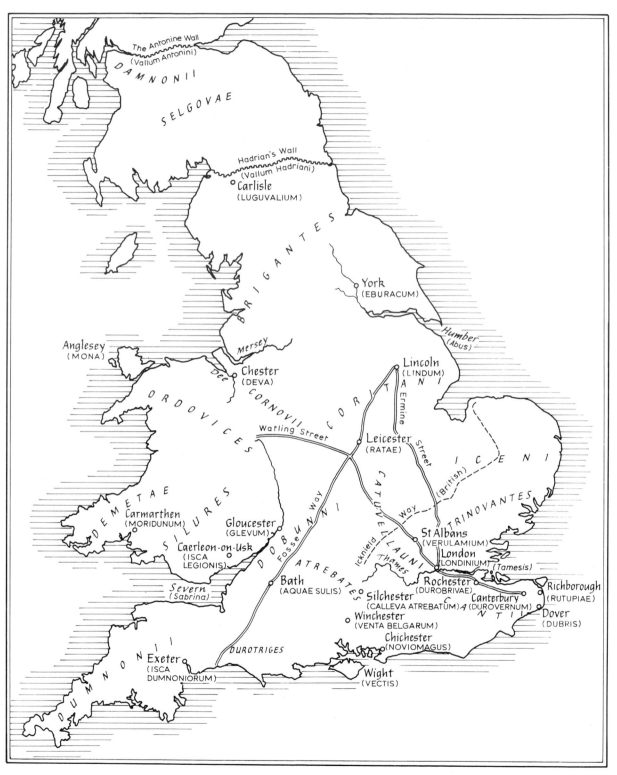

Roman Britain

HISTORICAL INTRODUCTION

'Real solemn history I cannot be interested in . . . the quarrels of popes and kings, with wars or pestilences in every page; the men all so good for nothing and hardly any women at all.' Catherine, Jane Austen's heroine in *Northanger Abbey,* would have found more to enjoy in Caxton's *The Description of Britain.* True there are few women mentioned, but there is at the same time nothing solemn about it. Despite appearances, William Caxton, the fifteenth-century printer and publisher, was not actually the author of the work: what Caxton chose to print in 1480 as *The Description of Britain* was, in fact, a small part of Ranulph Higden's Latin *Polychronicon* (literally, many stories), selected by Caxton from John Trevisa's translation of the first book of the *Polychronicon. The Description of Britain* was a compilation: almost a miscellany of information which might be of interest to English readers. It is a mixture of fact and fiction, of myth and legend, of knowledge and of invented explanations for the inexplicable. It was drawn from a number of sources, the reliability of which is discussed below. Caxton's selection is fascinating because it tells us what he, an astute businessman, thought English readers wanted to know; it gives us an idea of what an intelligent and literate late medieval Englishman or woman knew of their country. It can teach the modern reader much about the information which formed the world picture of medieval English men and women, much about their conception of the history, geography and traditions of their country.

When an Englishman in the later Middle Ages wanted to know about the past of his country there were several popular books to which he could turn. One was the *Brut,* a verse chronicle originally written in French to entertain an aristocratic audience. It began with the legendary story of Troy, but it was continued by various chroniclers who recorded the events of their own periods until, by the late fifteenth century (when it too was printed by Caxton) it covered the period up to the accession of Edward IV in 1461. From about 1330 it was one of a growing number of works available in English, and it very quickly became a popular work of English history. Illustrations from a fourteenth-century French version can be seen on pages

86, 88 and 108. That on page 108 shows the baptism of King Ethelbert of Kent, in 597, and it demonstrates to us one important fact about late medieval ideas of the past: it was not conceived as being very different in type to the present – the figures in this scene are dressed in fourteenth-century garments, down to the fashionable pointed shoes, not late sixth-century clothes. Similarly, the late fifteenth-century illustration on page 83 of the Dark Ages battle of Mount Badon, between the British semi-legendary King Arthur and the invading Saxon tribes, show the combatants all wearing stylish and up-to-date armour.

The *Brut* provided English readers with a versified account of their history. The other main source for the past was more scholarly in origin – the *Polychronicon,* written originally in Latin by a man who was perhaps the most knowledgeable and most well read of all the chroniclers of the period, Ranulph Higden, a monk at St Werburg's Monastery in Chester. Originally his work would have circulated primarily in monastic circles, but its fame grew quickly and the *Polychronicon* became widely popular, so much so that in 1352 Higden was summoned by Edward III to appear at the royal court. The popularity of medieval works in the days before printing can be measured by the number of manuscripts which survive; such a yardstick reinforces other evidence for the popularity of the *Polychronicon* which continued to be widely read until Tudor times. The dissemination of this work was increased from 1387, when an Oxford scholar, John Trevisa, translated it into English, explaining that he had found Higden's Latin difficult to read, '. . .Though I can speke, rede and understande Latyn, there is moche Latyn in these bookes of Cronykes that I cannot understande.'

The purpose of history in medieval eyes was threefold – to instruct, to entertain and to satisfy curiosity. Higden's *Polychronicon,* upon which the text of Caxton's *Description of Britain* was based, fulfilled all three criteria. To many Christian writers in the Middle Ages, history was universal, a record of the acts of God in the past, yet in practice historical works were usually less ambitious, more localized: most chroniclers were concerned first and foremost with local, regional and national events, perhaps preceding their works with a synopsis of world history in a crude attempt to give their writing a pedigree. Higden's *Polychronicon* was different; more truly universal. A compendium drawn from a wide range of sources, 'historical' is too narrow a term to apply to it, for it comprises geographical and topographical information, architectural descriptions, nuggets of historical information, stories of miracles and wonders. The *Polychronicon* treated the whole of world history from its beginnings through the Roman period down to the unification of the Roman classical tradition with the Christian tradition.

As the monk in charge of the monastic library and *scriptorium* (writing room) at the Benedictine monastery of St Werburg in Chester, Higden had access to a vast number of manuscripts. The greatest medieval libraries were to be found in monasteries which were the custodians of knowledge throughout the Middle Ages. The Benedictine order, to which Ranulph Higden belonged, emphasized reading and spiritual exercises, and about four hours a day might be spent by the monks reading, copying and illuminating manuscripts. A meeting of the governing body of the Benedictines in 1277 ordered the monks 'to study, write, correct, illuminate and bind books according to their capacities rather than labour in the fields'. This ruling, made not long before Ranulph Higden's birth, must have both encouraged the copying of books which were to be of use to him and also enabled him to have time to compile his great work. Higden's interest was in the origins of Britain: he was not interested in contemporary fourteenth-century society; he writes nothing of the Hundred Years War, of Edward I's campaigns against the Scots and Welsh, of the deposition of Edward II – all these events occurred during his lifetime but were not of interest to him; his concern was with the distant past.

At the same time, some comments which appear in the text tell us about contemporary medieval life. An 'R' in the margin of Ranulph's original text marks the pieces he had inserted into his compilation of sources. Additionally, when Trevisa translated Higden's work into English in the 1380s he produced a somewhat free translation which included a number of 'asides', casting light on some aspects of fourteenth-century life. Hardly surprisingly, these asides relate primarily to matters in which Trevisa himself was particularly interested. Trevisa was fascinated by Higden's description of the languages, manners and customs of the inhabitants of Britain (now chapter 15). Higden's comment on his own day '. . as people from the back of beyond want to ape and imitate gentlemen, they put a lot of effort into speaking French in order to be esteemed more highly' is reminiscent of Chaucer's description of the socially prestigious, archaic Anglo-French spoken by the haughty prioress in the prologue to *The Canterbury Tales,* ('And she spoke French very graciously and elegantly, in the Stratford-atte-Bowe style, since she was unfamiliar with Parisian French'). Trevisa's comment refers to a change which came about in England after the great plague epidemic, commonly known as the Black Death, struck England in 1348, a change which marks one of the major developments in English educational practice in the later Middle Ages – the teaching of children through the medium of English rather than French. Trevisa's final comment about the disadvantages of this change rings true, even to a twentieth-century reader: '. . . now they neither learn nor know any French which is a hindrance for people who have to travel overseas'. The illustration on page 113 shows two scenes of school life in the fifteenth century, and the text in this fifteenth-century picture laments a state of affairs again familiar today – the lack of knowledge among contemporary students, of grammar, described as 'the foundation and the beginning of knowledge'.

Caxton in his epilogue explained that he had included information about Ireland in *The Description,* . . .because Ireland is under English rule and has remained so for a very long time. . .'. Much of the historical information about Ireland is taken from the observations of Gerald of Wales who paid two visits to the country at the end of the twelfth century, shortly after it had come under the rule of the English kings. As to how reliable the extracts of text taken from Gerald of Wales are, the material relating to the Viking period and beyond is reasonably accurate. In England the Viking invaders and settlers had mostly been Danes, but Gerald correctly states that in Ireland the Norwegians formed the core of Viking settlers, and that they were responsible for the development of towns there. He is accurate also in his statements that Irish kings were not anointed, as was the case at the coronation of English and continental rulers, but succeeded each other

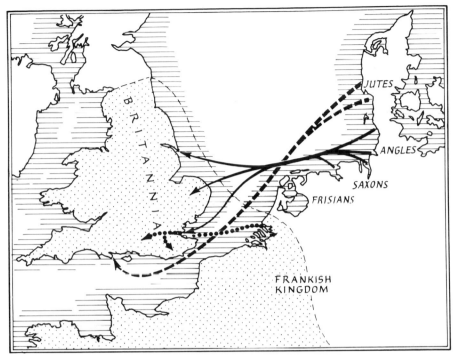

The Germanic invasions of Britain in the fifth and sixth centuries

primarily by force. His descriptions of the Irish were based partially at least on personal observations and his remarks concerning such matters as the lack of stirrups among Irish horsemen, and the fact that young babies were not swaddled as was the norm elsewhere, have been treated with respect by historians.

The text and the accompanying illustrations in this edition help to illuminate social and agrarian customs in England, In chapter three. ('Britain's Excellence and Attributes'), it is claimed that in some parts of Britain fish were so abundant that even swine were fed upon them. The illustration on page 35 shows two peasants knocking acorns down from trees for their pigs. Acorns were the normal food for pigs and this practice was so common that patches of woodland were often measured in terms of the number of pigs which could be supported there. Thus in Domesday Book, the woodland at Chelsea is described not in terms of linear measurements but as 'land for 60 pigs'.

Caxton's *Description* also refers to Domesday Book, William the Conqueror's great survey of land-owning and agricultural resources which can still be seen today in the Public Record Office Museum. This survey was so comprehensive that it provoked horror among the people – a common response in any age to the appearance of government officials on an investigation which might lead to an increase in taxation. One Anglo-Saxon chronicler commented that 'so very carefully he had it [England] investigated that there was not a single hide [land measurement]. . .nor even an ox nor a cow nor a pig that was overlooked and not included in the record'. Although printed four hundred years after the survey had been made, Caxton's *Description* preserves an impression of the huge scale of the survey. 'King William the Conqueror had all these provinces and shires surveyed and measured: in his time there were to be found thirty-six-and-a-half shires, fifty-two thousand and eighty towns, forty-five thousand and two parish churches, sixty thousand and fifteen knights' fiefs, of which men in orders possessed twenty-eight thousand and fifteen fiefs' (see page 76). The figures, despite their apparent precision, are wildly exaggerated, a common fault of medieval chroniclers, but none the less the impression is correct: the surveying of England in 1086 was a massive undertaking.

The Description also preserves a record of the 'harrying' of the North of England by William the Conqueror which had been provoked by an Anglo-Saxon and Danish rebellion there in 1069–70. William burned the countryside and destroyed villages so that future rebels and invading fleets would find nothing to live off. According to *The Description,* York '. . .looked as beautiful as Rome until King William the Conqueror destroyed it and the surrounding countryside with fire and flame, so that a pilgrim seeing it now would weep if he had known it in former days' (see page 66). Again, these exaggerated statements preserve a memory, albeit a rather blurred one, of the historical reality.

The text of *The Description* was a well tried one when Caxton came to print it. Yet, while on the one hand his printing of *The Description* (and subsequently the whole of Ranulph's *Polychronicon*) was the end of an era, it also marked the beginning of a new era. Within Caxton's own lifetime, partly due to the dissemination of works about the history of Britain, a new antiquarian curiosity was growing up, a desire to discover more about the material remains of the past, both natural and man-made. With the growth of Renaissance curiosity, it was no longer enough to dismiss strange phenomena as miraculous. Such interests were hinted at in parts of *The Description*, where, for example, Stonehenge was described (pages 41, 42–3) in the chapter on Britain's marvels and wonders, '. . . there are great and marvellously massive stones raised up like gateways, giving the appearance of one gateway set on top of another. Nonetheless it is neither apparent nor clearly understood how and why they are set up and balanced so miraculously.' William Worcester, an older contemporary of Caxton, carried sheets of paper in his saddle-bag as he rode about Britain in order to record places of interest and note curiosities. The resulting *Itinerary* displays both the range of his interests and the precision with which he carried out his observations – at old St Paul's Cathedral in London, for example, he paced out the length and width of the cathedral and recorded his findings.

Sixteenth-century scholars, their enthusiasm fired by the traditions of the history of Britain, followed up and developed these interests, often struggling to reconcile a conflict between common sense and the realities they saw around them and the semi-legendary traditions of the early history of Britain. Explorations of the new world and the discovery of primitive peoples there helped also in the forming of views of the past. From the 1560s representations of Red Indians were available in England, and the illustration of the Picts (seen here on page 105) was much influenced by this. Antiquarian pursuits, which from the sixteenth century onwards did much to develop people's interest in Britain's past, must have been stimulated by the work done by Caxton, Wynkyn de Worde and other early printers in making available the traditional works of English historical writings.

THE HISTORICAL SOURCES OF
THE DESCRIPTION OF BRITAIN

Ranulph Higden drew on the work of many authors in compiling his *Polychronicon* and references to his sources were retained in Caxton's

POWYS — Celtic
WESSEX — Germanic

STRATHCLYDE

BERNICIA
NORTHUMBRIA
DEIRA

ELMET

LINDSEY

GWYNEDD

WREOCEN-
SAETE

MERCIA

MIDDLE
ANGLIA

EAST
ANGLIA

POWYS

DYFED

MAGON-
SAETE
HWICCE

ESSEX

WESSEX

KENT

SUSSEX

DUMNONIA

The Anglo-Saxon kingdoms, c. AD 600

Description. In particular he quoted Bede, Alfred of Beverley, William of Malmesbury, Geoffrey of Monmouth and Gerald of Wales. I will attempt here to give a brief biographical account of these authors and an assessment of their historical worth. In brief, of the sources on which *The Description* relies, the parts of the work which are attributed to the writings of Geoffrey of Monmouth and Alfred of Beverley are romanticized constructs and are largely fictitious; the works of other writers are generally more reliable although it must be remembered that they contain a blend of oral traditions and personal observations as well as more formal historical material.

Gildas (*c.* 490–570): The very brief reference to Gildas in the text of *The Description* belies his importance as the first Briton to write history. In the century after the Romans withdrew from Britain, the country was invaded and settled by a number of Germanic tribes, including the Angles and the Saxons. Gildas, a Christian Celt from West Britain, provides us with our only written knowledge of this formative period in the history of the nation. His work, *The Ruin of Britain,* chronicles the invasions of these tribes and their wars against the native British. Gildas' writings were known in the Middle Ages, but the real historical information they provided was often ignored in favour of the more exciting, romanticized, legendary history of Britain devised in the twelfth century by Geoffrey of Monmouth (see below).

Bede (*c.* 673–735): The 'Venerable' Bede began his monastic career early. The presentation of young children to a monastery by their parents was a common practice in the early Middle Ages, and aged only seven Bede was sent to the flourishing Northumbrian monastery at Wearmouth, later moved to nearby Jarrow. Bede appears to have thrived under this system; he himself wrote that 'his special delight was always to learn, to teach and to write. . . .' Write he certainly did, becoming a prolific author of biblical commentaries, histories and lives of saints. His *Ecclesiastical History,* finished 731, was widely read in England and on the Continent throughout the middle ages. Like all his works, it had been written in Latin but in the ninth century King Alfred ordered its translation into English.

Bede wrote in a lively and vivid style. Today historians treasure his writings because of their valuable accounts of early English history, in particular of the conversion of the Anglo-Saxons to Christianity. Bede's *Ecclesiastical History* was popular in the Middle Ages for different reasons. Although written as a pious work for the edification of his audience, it included much secular as well as religious history. The two were very much intertwined. Bede attempted to explain history and to put events in a geographical setting; his work was enjoyed throughout the Middle Ages as a record of Anglo-Saxon achievements. It is the geographical element, the description of areas of the British Isles, rather than his vivid accounts of the Christianization of the English, which are most apparent in Caxton's *Decription of Britain.*

William of Malmesbury (*c.* 1095–*c.* 1143): Born less than thirty years after the Norman Conquest of England, William of Malmesbury must have been typical of many of his contemporaries in that one parent was English, the other Norman. His writings drew on both the Anglo-Saxon and Norman historical traditions. Like Bede, William was a prolific writer and a true historian. He too had been sent to a monastery at an early age, in his case the Benedictine house at Malmesbury in Wiltshire.

William saw the art of history as involving three things – investigation, craftsmanship and good story-telling. Although he was prepared, when he felt it necessary, to invent dialogue to give his stories veracity, he was keen to reconstruct the past as accurately as he could, to record the truth about people and events for the edification and entertainment of his audience. His works include *Deeds of the Kings of England, Deeds of the Archbishops and Bishops of the English, A Recent History* (covering the period 1128–42). As librarian of the monastery at Malmesbury, he had access to numerous manuscripts. Some of the sources he used for the Anglo-Saxon period have since been lost and we know of them only through his references. He did not restrict his attention to manuscripts for, unlike Bede who rarely left his monastery at Jarrow,

William of Malmesbury travelled widely. He made use in his histories of what he observed on his travels and was the first historian in England to make extensive use of topography (the siting of man-made and natural objects in the landscape) and ancient monuments as historical records. This aspect of his writings appears in Caxton's *Description* as do many of his comments on the Norman Conquest of England.

Geoffrey of Monmouth (*c.* 1100–1154): Geoffrey of Monmouth was almost certainly born in Wales, perhaps of a Breton family. He may well have been born near Caerleon-on-Usk, near Monmouth, which is referred to regularly in his writings. Much of his adult life was spent in Oxford, (not yet a flourishing university city), and later in London, but towards the end of his life he returned to Wales, becoming bishop of the little Welsh see of St Asaph in 1152.

The previous authors mentioned all had a dual purpose in their writings; they wished both to instruct and to entertain their readers. Geoffrey of Monmouth's primary aim was entertainment. By the mid twelfth century, romance literature, which emphasized and glorified warfare, battles, heroism and great men, was very fashionable and Geoffrey's *History of the Kings of Britain* was aimed at an audience which looked for this. His *History of the Kings of Britain* was very much a romanticized history which was to provide a fruitful mine for the imagination of other later writers. Geoffrey tried to give his work an air of historical authenticity by claiming that it was based on a lost Breton work; he claims at the beginning of the book that 'Walter, archdeacon of Oxford, a man skilled in the art of public speaking and well informed about the history of foreign countries, presented me with a certain very ancient book written in the British language. This book, attractively composed to form a consecutive and orderly narrative, set out all the deeds of these men, from Brutus, the first king of the Britons, down to Cadwallader, the son of Cadwallo. At Walter's request I have taken the trouble to translate the book into Latin.' Geoffrey's book, however, is not the reputable historical work that his preface implied. It is a legendary history which purports to

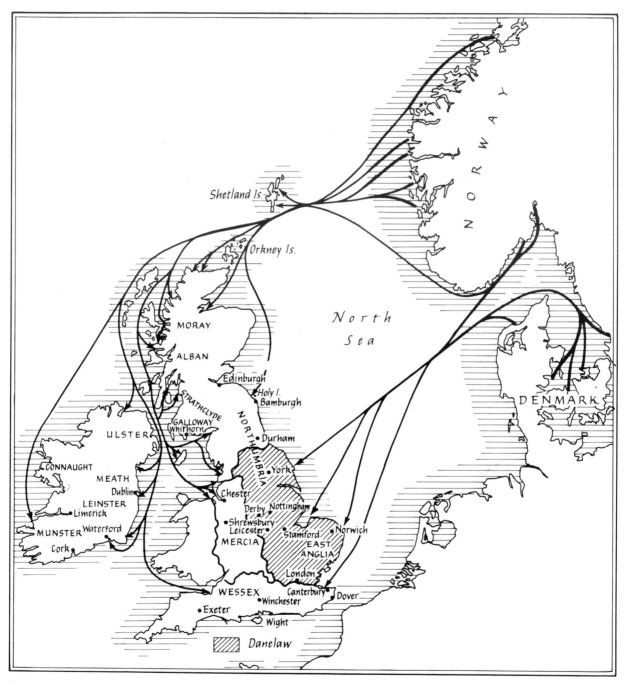

The Danish invasions and the Danelaw

cover the period from prehistoric times to the late seventh century . Brutus, who dominates the early part of Geoffrey's work and who continues to figure in Caxton's *Description,* was an imaginary figure. The whole work is a mixture of fact, drawn from other writers, and fiction – a combination which makes it difficult to establish the degree of truth in it. It was none the less popular for that; it was among the 'bestsellers' of its day, translated and summarized in English, Welsh and Anglo-Norman and existing now in numerous manuscripts. Its popularity was due largely to its glorified and patriotic view of British history. Geoffrey glorified the Britons and denigrated the Anglo-Saxons and the contemporary Welsh, an attitude which endeared him to his Anglo-Norman audience who had conquered Britain by defeating the Anglo-Saxons in 1066. From the late twelfth century until the early sixteenth century Geoffrey's account of the early history of Britain was accepted by most people as true and it greatly influenced later authors. His work featured in Higden's *Polychronicon* and thus also in Caxton's *Description.*

Alfred of Beverley (mid twelfth century): Alfred of Beverley is a far less well-known figure than the other writers whose work contributed to *The Description.* He was treasurer of Beverley Minster, an important ecclesiastical site which lies between Hull and York. Beverley is marked on the very early map of the area north of the Humber shown on page 58. His chronicle was copied primarily from the work of Geoffrey of Monmouth and is thus of little independent value. Clearly Ranulph Higden had a manuscript of Alfred's work to hand when he wrote the *Polychronicon* for Alfred of Beverley is fairly frequently cited despite the lack of any real additional material in his work.

Gerald of Wales (*c.* 1145–1214): Gerald of Wales was one of the great raconteurs of the middle ages, a colourful figure with a witty, entertaining and often vitriolic pen. He hoped, through his works, to gain the favour of important and influential men and thus rise within the church, an ambition which despite the popularity of his works was thwarted, leaving him by the end of his life, rather embittered. Gerald was a secular cleric who travelled widely in England, Wales, Ireland and on the continent. He had studied in Paris, one intellectual centre of his age; he was also connected with another of the most exciting and stimulating intellectual centres of his time, the court of King Henry II. His writings are based on first-hand experience and travel, on stories told to him on his travels and on his personal observation. His descriptions of Ireland and Wales formed the basis for the relevant sections of *The Description of Britain;* his fascination with and sharp eye for detail make his comments on Ireland and Wales of particular interest to the social historian. He himself states that he concentrated on Ireland and Wales partly because he felt that they had been neglected by previous writers.

Gerald blended oral and literary sources together, and added his own perceptive observations to produce a literary narrative which would tell a good story, but he was well able to distinguish truth from hearsay, writing in his *Topography of Ireland* that '. . .it is only when he who reports a thing is also the one that witnessed it that anything is established on the sound basis of truth'. Much of the subtlety of the text is lost in *The Description of Britain* as printed by Caxton for it had been copied by Higden, then again by Trevisa and finally by Caxton. Summarizing leads to inaccuracies and this work is no exception. To take a single example, the statement found in Caxton's *Description,* page 153, that after the Flood, Bartolanus, son of Sere, who was descended from Noah's son Japhet went to Ireland with his three sons. What Gerald of Wales actually said is that Bartolanus '. . .is said to have been brought there' which places quite a different interpretation on matters. However the form in which Caxton printed it is how many late medieval readers would have known Gerald's writings and thus, this is how they would have perceived the past through his eyes. Of all the authors referred to in *The Description of Britain,* Gerald would have been the most delighted by the notion of a printing press making multiple copies and bringing fame to writers; he was not shy about promoting his own image.

Virginia Davis
Westfield College (University of London)

FURTHER READING

About medieval historical writing:

A. Gransden, *Historical Writing in England c. 550 – c. 1307* (Routledge & Kegan Paul, 1974)

A. Gransden, *Historical Writing in England c. 1307 to the early 16th century* (Routledge & Kegan Paul, 1982)

B. Smalley, *Historians in the Middle Ages* (Thames & Hudson, 1974)

J. Taylor, *English Historical Literature in the Fourteenth Century* (OUP, 1987)

Editions of sources cited in *The Description:*

Gildas, *The Ruin of Britain,* translated and edited by M. Winterbottom (Phillimore, 1978)

Bede, *A History of the English Church and People,* translated and edited by L. Sherley-Price (Penguin, 1968)

Gerald of Wales, *The Journey through Wales and the Description of Britain,* translated and edited by L. Thorpe (Penguin, 1978)

Gerald of Wales, *The History and Topography of Ireland,* translated and edited by J. O'Meara (Penguin, 1982)

Geoffrey of Monmouth, *The History of the Kings of Britain,* translated and edited by L. Thorpe (Penguin, 1966)

EDITOR'S INTRODUCTION

illiam Caxton, Britain's first printer and publisher, was born some time between 1415 and 1421. The earlier part of his career was spent as a mercer and merchant-adventurer and he was based in the Low Countries. From his observation of the Continental book trade, he saw how the needs of an entirely new market of readers could be met by what the latest printing technology had to offer. So, during a stay in Cologne, he acquired the skills and equipment of a printer and began publishing in 1476, first in Bruges and then back home at Westminster. With the lifelong faithful assistance of Wynkyn de Worde, an Alsatian who settled in England as his right-hand man, Caxton was able to engage in activities over and above the more mechanical ones of book production, acting as redactor, editor, and bookseller, as he felt necessary.

Caxton was first and foremost a businessman; he needed books to be saleable if he was to earn his living. *The Description of Britain* was an astute choice, as it was a considerable success. Caxton saw how he could meet a contemporary need; he was aware of people's curiosity about their world and their need for attractively packaged information. In his Preface Caxton says he is printing the *Description* because, although the chronicles of England are widely available (indeed, recently put into print by Caxton himself), knowledge of the 'nobility and excellence' of Britain is not as widespread as it should be. In his Epilogue he goes so far as to say that it is 'necessary for all Englishmen to know the special nature, endowments and marvels' of the British Isles. Five centuries later, we still have an emotional as well as an intellectual 'need to know', to judge from the popularity of illustrated books and television programmes on the history, architecture and natural history of our own and other countries.

More people in the late fifteenth century could read and, in particular, those in the middle to upper social brackets had the leisure to do so. This broadened reading public consisted of laymen (and quite a few women too), not clergymen, with lively preoccupations with this world as well as a duly pious concern for the destiny of their souls in the next. Entertainment and instruction, particularly when the instruction was socially advantageous, went down well. In the case of *The Description of Britain*, Caxton's business sense paid off: two years later, presumably on the strength of the book's success, he printed the whole *Polychronicon*, from which the *Description* was taken, in Trevisa's translation.

Between 1476 and 1491 (the year of his death), Caxton continued to print what the public wanted. This included works by the poets Chaucer, Gower, and Lydgate, romances such as Sir Thomas Malory's *Le Morte Darthur*, the 'Reynard the Fox' stories in Caxton's own translation from the Dutch, religious works suitable for leisured devotion, and works of instruction such as *The Book of Good Manners* and *The Game and Play of the Chess*, useful to those aiming for upward social mobility.

Very few medieval books could be described as the work of only one author. Caxton was the first to acknowledge his debt for *The Description of Britain* (1480) to two previous scholars: Ranulph Higden, an early fourteenth-century monk of Chester and author of the Latin *Polychronicon* or 'Universal History'; and John Trevisa, the later fourteenth-century translator of that work into Middle English. It was perfectly respectable – even recommended medieval practice – for an author to take his material from some pre-existing literary source and to re-work it, lengthening or shortening it to suit his literary purpose. Modern scandals and lawsuits about literary plagiarism would have struck Caxton and his contemporaries as eccentric. Indeed, an acknowledgment of the respected authorities on which a new work depended gave it added weight and status. Thus, in his Epilogue, Caxton tells us: 'I have taken [*The Description of Britain*] out of the *Polychronicon* and . . . I have set [it] in print according to the translation of Trevisa.' In any case Ranulph Higden could scarcely have cast the first stone, as his work is a well-woven tissue of materials from many sources. In the sections on the British Isles we find citations of Saint Augustine,[1] Paulus Orosius,[2] Isidore of Seville,[3] the Venerable Bede,[4] Alfred of Beverley,[5] William of Malmesbury,[6] Geoffrey of Monmouth[7] and Gerald of Wales,[8] to name only the major figures.

However, authority was not immune to criticism. When John Trevisa came to translate the *Polychronicon* into Middle English during the later fourteenth century, he felt free to add acid comments on the pronouncements of some of Ranulph's authorities. For example, Caxton has retained his tart observation in Chapter Nine that 'if Gerald of Wales was doubtful whether or not it was permissible to believe this, it was scarcely a prudent course to record it in his books, as some people would point out, for it is a remarkable delusion to write a long history to record things permanently for posterity whilst still remaining uncertain whether one's belief is misplaced.'

In printing *The Description of Britain*, Caxton was not 'pirating' John Trevisa's translation in any modern sense. He took only a comparatively small proportion of the whole *Polychronicon* (which deals with not just British, but world history and geography, in seven long books), rearranging the chapters on England, Wales, Scotland and Ireland from Book I into a logical order to produce a coherent structure. He starts with the British mainland: England, Wales, and Scotland, and ends with Ireland, which, though separate from the mainland, he includes 'because [it] is under English rule and has remained so for a very long time'. Caxton's work as editor and redactor shows that he paid close attention to small-scale as well as large-scale aspects of the job. He omitted and rephrased material for clarity, substituting more modern fifteenth-century vocabulary and constructions for words and phrases which had gone out of date in the hundred or so years between Trevisa's translation and his own reworking.

Caxton always wanted to be comprehensible and clear. Of the *Polychronicon* he says: '[I] somewhat have changed the rude and old English, that is to wit, certain words which in these days be neither used nor understood.' Much of *The Description of Britain* is perfectly comprehensible to a modern audience, though, as for its medieval counterpart, there might be problems with 'certain words which in these days be neither used nor understood' without glosses. Faced with this disorientating version of the perennial problem of the translator, and dissatisfied with the results of half-measures in modernization (such as simply normalizing the spelling), I decided in effect to rewrite the *Description* to be readily comprehensible to a twentieth-century audience. This has involved making decisions about interpretation and occasional silent expansion which cannot be discussed in detail in a book of this kind. For those who would like to look behind the scenes, many of these decisions will be illuminated by consulting the equivalent chapters on the British Isles in the full *Polychronicon* available in the Rolls Series (volumes 41:1 and 41:2), where Higden's Latin, Trevisa's translation (with annotations indicating where the 1482 full Caxton print differs from it) and an independent anonymous fifteenth-century translation are available.

As there is no modern scholarly edition available of the 1480 *Description*, this illustrated version brings Caxton's translation into the twentieth century for the first time. This rendering is based on my transcription of the copy in the British Library. I have attempted to represent Caxton's meaning as far as possible, consulting Higden's Latin and Trevisa's Middle English throughout; and on occasions small amounts of explanatory material have been built into my text. These do not, I think, betray the purposes of any of the authors whose work has gone into the making of the *Description* (indeed, John Trevisa was quite happy to build in explanatory glosses, sometimes so repetitively that one feels one could do without them, though Caxton apparently did not feel this, as he has retained them). I have provided more extensive explanations in numbered footnotes. Though every attempt has been made to render the meaning accurately, no responsibility is taken for the 'accuracy' (in the modern sense) of the topographical, botanical, zoological and other information offered in good faith by the many authorities quoted, nor am I responsible for the scathing contempt (much of it borrowed from Gerald of Wales) with which various races and tribes are treated!

Marie Collins
Westfield College (University of London)

William Caxton's monogram

PREFACE AND TABLE OF CONTENTS

t is the case that in many and various places the common chronicles of England are obtainable and have recently been printed at Westminster. And since the description of this island, which in bygone times was called Albion and, later, Britain, has not been produced and is not commonly obtainable, and its nobility and excellence are not well known, I therefore intend to give in this book the description of Britain and its attributes.

Chapter One

THE NAMES OF BRITAIN

s Geoffrey of Monmouth says, this island was called Albion after Albina, the Emperor Diocletian's eldest daughter,[1] who had thirty-two sisters. They were the first inhabitants of this country. As some chronicles record, Albina called this country Albion after herself, because she was the eldest sister. According to others, this country was called Albion, as if to say 'the white land', because of the white sea-cliffs around the coast which were visible from far away. Later, Brutus[2] conquered this country and called it Britain after himself.

Then the Saxons, or English,[3] conquered this country and called it

This map of Europe, dating from 1490, shows the contours, though not the proportions, recognizable to the modern eye, with Britain placed as 'an angle or corner of the world'

Matthew Paris, a monk of St Albans and a notable artist, drew this map, one of the earliest of Great Britain extant, c. 1250

Anglia, that is, England. Alternatively, it was called Anglia after a queen called Angela, who ruled this country and was the daughter of a noble Saxon duke. Or again, by Isidore's[4] account, Anglia takes its name from being like an angle or corner of the world. Bede[5] offers yet another explanation: St Gregory saw English children for sale in Rome, and he granted that the name of the country was appropriate and said: 'They are truly angels, for their faces shine like those of angels,' for the nobility of the land shone in the children's faces. According to Alfred of Beverley,[6] Britain (or Anglia) is called 'the second world', and for the great abundance of all its good things Charlemagne[7] called it his 'own chamber'. Alfred explains that this island is called *insula*, or 'island' in Latin, because it is *in salo*: 'in the sea', and it is continually beaten by various currents, streams, and waves.

Chapter Two

BRITAIN'S LOCATION, BOUNDARIES AND DIMENSIONS

ritain is considered to be a noble land in both our histories and those of the Greeks. It is set opposite Germany, France, and Spain, between the north and the west, with the sea in between. This country is fifty miles from Gessorico,[1] the cliff of the race known as the Morini. Bede says that because this island lies near the north extremity of the world, it has light, bright nights in the summertime, so that often at midnight people debate and are uncertain whether it is evening or daybreak (that is, during the period of the year when the sun does not go very far beneath the earth at night, but travels around the northern edge and quickly returns to the east). Therefore, in summer there are very long days of eighteen hours, with nights of six hours, and afterwards in winter there are long nights of eighteen hours and short days of six hours. Some further information: in Armenia, Macedonia, Italy, and other countries in similar positions, the longest day, like the longest night, is fifteen hours long, and the shortest day, like the shortest night, is

This view of an inhabited medieval landscape appeared as the frontispiece to a later reprint of The Description of Britain *by Caxton's assistant and heir, Wynkyn de Worde, in 1498*

Perhaps England's most famous landmark, the white cliffs near Dover, which gave rise to the notion that the country's alternative name, Albion, was derived from the Latin albus, *'white'*

A twelfth-century illustration of the eighth-century monk and historian, the Venerable Bede, from whom many of the geographical and topographical observations in The Description of Britain *are derived*

nine hours long. Pliny[2] relates that in Meroe,[3] the principal island of black people, the longest day lasts twelve hours; in Alexandria in Egypt it is thirteen hours; in Italy it lasts fifteen hours; in the island called Thule[4] all the six summer months are daylight and all the six winter months are night.

According to Isidore of Seville, Britain is set opposite France and Spain within Ocean, the sea surrounding the earth, as if it were beyond the limits of the world. Gerald of Wales describes Britain as set lengthways, being wider in the middle than at the ends. Orosius[5] says that Britain stretches lengthways from south to north, and to the south-east it has France, to the south, Spain, to the north, Norway, and to the west, Hibernia or Ireland. When sailors pass the nearest cliff of the land they see a city called 'Rutpimouth', which according to Bede has now been corrupted to 'Reptachester', now Richborough. By Solinus's[6] account, Britain is eight hundred miles long, if it is measured from the cliff of Totnes to the point of Caledonia; or by Alfred's account, from Penwithstreet (fifteen miles beyond Michaelstow in Cornwall) to Caithness at the far extremity of Scotland; and Britain is over two hundred miles wide from Menevia, the most far-flung place in Wales, to Yarmouth in Norfolk. Bede excepts the longest projections of various promontories; but if they are included, Britain is forty-eight times seventy thousand paces all around its perimeter.

Chapter Three

BRITAIN'S EXCELLENCE AND ATTRIBUTES

s France surpasses Britain, so Britain surpasses Ireland in good weather and splendour, but not in health-giving qualities. Bede observes that Britain is pre-eminent in bringing forth trees, fruit, cattle and beasts, and in some places, vines grow. The land has an abundance of birds and beasts of various species, and it is productive, as is the sea. The country is splendid, richly abundant in excellent wells and rivers full of fish. There is a great abundance of small fish, salmon, and eels, so that, according to William of Malmesbury, in some places the people feed their swine with fish. Bede says that dolphins, sea-calves and baleens (huge fish like whales) are often caught, as are various kinds of shellfish, including mussels which contain pearls of all sorts of colours and shades: reddish, red-purple and blue; and most particularly, white. There are also many shellfish which are used to dye things a fine red; this redness is marvellously beautiful and stable, never discolouring with

Fish featured on the menu of some swine in medieval days. Others – like the ones in this early fourteenth-century picture, from Queen Mary's Psalter in the British Library – had to put up with acorns

An angler profiting from Britain's 'rivers full of fish'. From Wynkyn de Worde's print of The Book of St Albans

cold, heat, wetness or dryness; rather, the older it is, the lovelier the colour. There are also salt springs and hot springs from which run streams for hot baths, directed to different places appointed for men and women of all ages, old or young. Basileus[1] says that the water which runs past veins of certain metals takes in great heat in its course. This island is rich in veins of metal such as brass, iron, lead, tin, and silver. Pliny relates that in this island, beneath its turf, there is good marl to be found; it is full of productive richness, so that the more thickly a field is covered with marl, the better the corn it will bear. There is also another kind of white marl, which improves land which is marled with it for eighty years.

According to Solinus, in this island there is found a stone called 'gagates' or jet. If you wish to know of its beauty, it is as black as jewels can be; if you are curious about its nature, it burns in water and is quenched in oil, and as for its powers, if the stone is heated by rubbing, it holds whatever comes near it, like a stone by the name of 'succins'. Isidore says that there are sheep that bear good wool. There are many harts and wild beasts, and few wolves, so

'Baked tiles for covering houses and churches' can be seen in this illustration of building the Tower of Babel, from a manuscript containing a translation of Genesis by the late tenth-century Anglo-Saxon monk Ælfric

that sheep are all the more safely left unwatched in the field. According to Ranulph, in this island there are in addition many beautiful, splendid, and rich cities and towns, many great rivers and streams with a great abundance of fish, and many large and lovely woods, with very many animals, both tame and wild. The soil of the country is rich in metal ores, salt springs, quarries of marble and various kinds of stone: red, white, soft and hard, chalk, and white lime. There are also red and white clays for making pots, crocks, stoneware, and other vessels as well as baked tiles for covering houses and churches as if in a second Samia or Samos.[2] Flanders[3] greatly prizes the wool of this country, and Holland[4] the skins and pelts of all kinds of animals, Gascony[5] its iron and lead, Ireland its ores and salt. All Europe loves and wishes for the

A late medieval woodcut depicting milk-churning: 'this island must surpass the rest in land, honey, milk and cheese'

Sowing winter wheat, the labour appropriate to the month of October, from a glass roundel from Coslany, Norwich, now in the Victoria and Albert Museum

Milking ewes, from an illustration in the early fourteenth-century East Anglian Luttrell Psalter. Ewe's milk was greatly valued for cheesemaking

white metal[6] of this land.

According to Alfred, Britain is sufficiently provided with the materials necessary for buying and selling or for people's use; neither salt nor iron is lacking. Therefore a poet praises this country in the following way in his verse:

England is a good land, rich in wool, though a corner of the world. England is full of pleasures and of noble people fully deserving enjoyment, fine men with noble tongues, noble hearts and everything about them noble. Their hands are more gracious and generous than their tongues. In addition, England is a beautiful country, flower of all surrounding countries. The land is very pleasantly endowed with its own fruits and products. It offers relief to foreigners in need, and when hunger afflicts other countries, it feeds them. The country is truly pleasant, whilst people live in peace. East and west, in every country, England's havens are well known. It is provided with ships which often help other countries. In it, people always hold their food and money much more in common, and they gladly give gifts in exchange for learning. Far and wide by land and sea people speak of England. This island must surpass the rest in land, honey, milk, and cheese. It has no need for other countries; they all have to ask for help from this one alone. King Solomon might well marvel at the delightfulness of this native land, and the Emperor Octavian[7] might well long for the riches it contains.

Chapter Four

BRITAIN'S MARVELS AND WONDERS

I n Britain there are hot wells, excellently fitted and appointed for the use of mankind. The presiding spirit of those wells is the great goddess Minerva.[1] In her dwelling endures perpetual fire that is never transformed into ashes, but as the fire abates it turns to clods of stone. Alfred says that there are many wonders in Britain, and yet four are the most wonderful of all. The first is at the Peak,[2] where such a strong wind blows out of the fissures of the earth that it flings back pieces of cloth which people throw into it. The second is at Stonehenge near Salisbury, where there are great and marvellously massive stones raised up like gateways, giving the appearance of one gateway set on top of another. Nonetheless it is neither apparent nor clearly understood how and why they are set up and balanced so miraculously. The third is at Cheddar where there is a great underground cavern. Many people have often

The rugged landscape of the Derbyshire Peak District, typified by this view of Lose Hill from Mam Tor

The dramatic and massive gate-like structures of Stonehenge. Their engineering puzzled Ranulph Higden, John Trevisa and William Caxton

St Æthelthryth, Etheldreda, or Audrey, from the Benedictional of St Æthelwold; the flowers she carries probably betoken her virginity

walked in it and have seen rivers and streams, but they cannot find an end to them anywhere. The fourth is that rain can be seen rising on hills and immediately falling in the fields.

There is also a great lake[3] containing sixty islands well fitted for people to inhabit; it is enclosed by a hundred and twenty rocks, on each of which is an eagle's nest. Sixty rivers run into the lake, only one of which flows into the sea. There is a lake enclosed by a wall of tiles and stone, in which people very often wash and bathe, each person feeling the water exactly as hot or as cold as he himself wishes. There are salt springs far from the sea which are salt all week long until noon on Saturday and fresh from then until Monday. When boiled, the water of these springs yields fine and beautiful white salt. There is also a lake containing water with a marvellous effect, for even if a whole army were to stand facing it, its water would draw them with violent force towards it, wetting all their clothing, and horses would be drawn in exactly the same way. Yet, if one's face is turned away from the water, it causes no trouble. There is a well neither fed by, nor feeding, any stream, yet four kinds of fish can be caught in it; it is only twenty feet in both length and breadth, and only knee-deep, surrounded on all sides by high banks.

In the country surrounding Winchester there is a hollow in the earth, or cavern, out of which a strong wind always blows, so that no one can stand outside it for any length of time. There is also a lake which turns wood into iron if it remains under the water for a year, so that pieces of wood are fashioned into whetstones. Again, on top of a hill there is a grave; everyone

An evening view of 'Pimblemere' or Lake Bala in North Wales, mentioned as the source of the River Dee. It was reputed to have magical powers

who comes and measures it will find it to be exactly his own length and size and, if a pilgrim kneels down by it, he will immediately be completely refreshed, feeling untroubled by weariness. In his 'Description', Gerald of Wales says that close to Wimborne Minster, not far from Bath, there is a wood bearing much fruit; if its trees fall into water or on to ground near water and lie there a whole year, they turn to stone. In his 'Journey', Gerald relates that at the foot of the city of Chester runs the River Dee which now forms the boundary between England and Wales. It changes its crossing-places every month. According to the local people, it often leaves its channel, and the people on the side it draws closer to in any year (England or Wales) will have the worst of it and be beaten that year, and the people on the other side will come out on top and beat them. It forebodes such events when the river changes its course in this way. The River Dee originates and flows from a lake called Pimblemere or Bala, and although the river contains a great abundance of salmon, there is never any to be found in that lake.

William of Malmesbury instructs us to take heed what great radiance and brightness of God's mercy has been vouchsafed to the English since they first turned to the true faith, so that amongst no people in any region are there found so many human bodies undecayed after death. This is a token of the everlasting life which is to come after the Day of Judgment. That appears plainly in the cases of these holy saints,[4] Audrey, King Edmund, Alphege, Edgar, Cuthbert, Edward and many another. I believe that it is brought about by the special grace of Almighty God, to the end that this nation, which is placed as if beyond the bounds of the world, should pay heed to the burial of bodies without corruption and rotting, and be all the more bold and steadfast in trusting, at the final resurrection of the dead, that they will live eternally after the Day of Judgment.

The Roman Baths – one example of the 'hot wells' mentioned in the text – at Aquae Sulis or Bath, presided over by Sul Minerva, a combination of a British and a Roman deity

A miracle of the royal saint Edmund (in answer to his prayer a spring appears); from a late fifteenth-century illustration of the poet John Lydgate's Life of St Edmund

Chapter Five

THE PRINCIPAL DIVISIONS OF BRITAIN

fter the time of Brutus, the first King of the Britons, the island of Britain began to be split into three principal divisions: Loegria; Cambria (which is Wales); and Albany (which is now Scotland). The name Loegria was derived from Locrinus, Brutus's eldest son, and was used as if to signify 'Locrinus's land', but now Loegria is called England. Its boundaries and limits were once the English Channel to both the east and the south, and according to Bede, to the north, two inlets of the sea cutting far inland opposite each other (they do not, however, meet). Of those two inlets, the eastern one begins about two

An aerial view of Offa's Dyke, giving a sense of the massiveness of this earthwork intended as 'a partition for all time between the Kings of England and Wales'

A portrait of King Offa from a coin now in the British Museum

miles from the monastery of Ebburcuring,[1] to the west of Penulton; on the inlet is a town called Guydy. The more westerly of the two inlets has, on its right side, a fortified city called Alcluid, which in the local language is called Cluidstone and which stands by a river also called Cluid.

Ranulph reports that some people would say Loegria ends at the Humber and stretches no further northwards. The second region of Britain is called Albany, that is, Scotland. It takes its name from Albanactus,[2] one of Brutus's sons, and stretches from the two inlets of the sea I have just mentioned northwards as far as the Sea of Norway. However, the southern regions of Albany (where the Picts once dwelt) stretch from the waters of the Tweed as far as the Scottish Sea. All that once belonged to Bernicia, the northern kingdom of Northumbria, from the earliest period of the English kings until the time when Kenneth McAlpine, King of Scotland, expelled the Picts, thereby annexing it to the kingdom of Scotland.

The third division of Britain is Wales or Wallia, also called Cambria; a name deriving from Camber, another of Brutus's sons, because he was Prince of Wales. To the east, the Severn once marked the boundary between England and Wales, but now, to the north, the River Dee at Chester, and to the south, the River Vaga at the castle of Strigelin, divide the two regions. In addition, King Offa,[3] in order to have a partition for all time between the

Kings of England and Wales, built a long dyke stretching from the south past Bristol, northwards along the edge of the Welsh mountains, following the rivers Severn and Dee almost to their sources and continuing to the mouth of the River Dee beyond Chester, close to Flint castle, reaching the sea between Colehill and the monastery of Basingwerk. This dyke is still to be seen in many places. In the time of King Edward, Welshmen were forbidden, on pain of severe punishment, to cross the dyke armed; this was brought about by the efforts of Earl Harold as you will hear later. Nowadays, however, on both this side and the far side of the dyke, and especially in Cheshire, Shropshire and Herefordshire, English people and Welsh people are intermingled in many places.

Chapter Six

THE ADJACENT ISLANDS

ritain has three adjacent islands belonging to it, not including the Orkneys, which correspond to the three divisions of Britain. The Isle of Wight belongs and lies adjacent to Loegria, that is, England; the island of Mon, also called Anglesey, belongs to Wales; and the island of Eubonia, known also by two other names, Menania and Man, belongs to Scotland. All these three island, Wight, Mon and Man, are of almost equal sizes and dimensions; we shall now give an account of them in succession.

By Bede's account, Claudius sent Vespasian[1] to conquer Wight, which stretches thirty miles from east to west and twelve from north to south, being distant six miles at its eastern end and three miles at its western end from the cliffs of the south coast of Britain. Again, Bede says that in the estimation of the English, the island contains one thousand two hundred households.

Gerald of Wales, in his 'Journey', relates that Mon, also called Anglesey, is separated from North Wales by a short inlet of the sea about two miles across. On Mon there are three hundred and sixty-three settlements estimated at three 'candreds' or 'hundreds'. (A 'candred' is the amount of

The Calf of Man, the smaller island adjacent to the Isle of Man; could it really have supported three hundred households?

land which will contain a hundred settlements; the term 'candred' is formed from two languages, British and Irish.) The island is approximately thirty miles long and twelve miles wide. In praise of this island Welshmen are accustomed to quote a proverb, '*Mon mam Kembry*' ('Mon mother of Wales' in English), meaning that the land is so good that it appears that it would provide enough corn for all the people of Wales. A piece of Virgil's[2] verse is appropriate to that:

> et quantum longis carpunt armenta diebus,
> exigua tantum gelidus ros nocte reponit

> [and all that the herds crop in the long daytimes
> the chill dew replenishes in the brief space of night].

In the straits separating the island from North Wales is a whirlpool which attracts and swallows up ships sailing past it, just like Scylla and Charybdis,[3] a pair of dangerous natural features in the Mediterranean. For this reason people cannot sail past this whirlpool when the tide is running high except with the utmost skill. Ranulph, on whose *Polychronicon* this book depends, says that information is to be found on the marvels and wonders of Anglesey in the chapter on Wales, which appears later in my version.

Gerald of Wales, in his 'Journey', says that the third island, known also as Eubonia and Menania, or Man, lies between Ulster in Ireland and Galloway in Scotland, just as if in the sea's navel. Bede describes the Isle of Man as containing in effect two islands. The first, to the south, encompasses a wider area and is better for growing corn; it contains nine hundred and sixty households. The second, in the estimation of Englishmen, has room for over three hundred. Gerald relates that there was once strife about whether this island should belong to Britain or Ireland; because poisonous snakes which

A late medieval woodcut of a witch creating a storm at sea. The text tells of witches on the Isle of Man, and to this day the island has a reputation for witchcraft

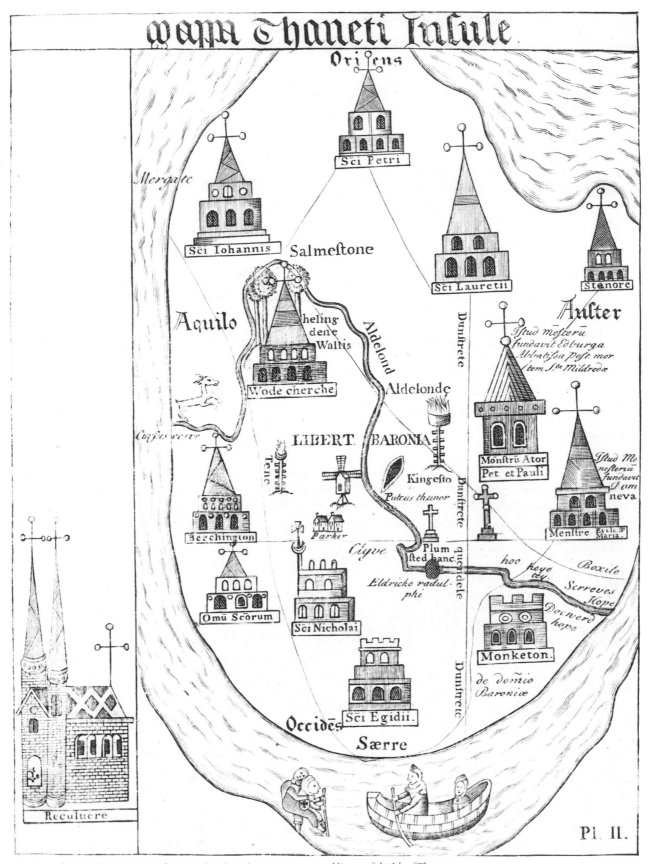

The island of Thanet off the Kent coast, from an early eighteenth-century antiquarian History of the Isle of Thanet

were taken there survived, it was adjudged that the Isle of Man should belong to Britain, as will be explained in a later chapter. Ranulph says that enchantment and witchcraft are practised on the island, for the women there sell wind to sailors, apparently tied up in three knots of twine; the more wind a man requires, the more knots he must undo. Often there, during the daytime, the inhabitants see people who have previously died going about headless or unharmed, and also the manner of their death. Foreigners place their feet on top of the feet of the inhabitants in order to see such sights as they do. According to Bede, the Scots were the first inhabitants of the island. Thanatos or Thanet is an island lying off Kent, and takes its name ('thanatos' meaning 'death' in Greek) from the death of snakes there, since there are none on the island; its soil, carried into other lands, kills snakes. It contains fine fruitful cornland. This island is held to have been hallowed and blessed by Saint Augustine,[4] the first Doctor of the Church to Englishmen, since he first landed there.

Chapter Seven

THE KING'S HIGHWAYS AND STREETS

oliuncius[1] was the thirteenth King of the Britons and the first to give them laws. He ordained that the ploughs of farmers, the temples of gods and the highways leading people to cities and towns, should possess the inviolability of sanctuary, so that everyone going to any of them for help or because of an offence he had committed should be safe against pursuit by all his enemies. Later, however, because the highways were uncertainly defined and disputes occurred, Belinus, the son of the Moliuncius we have just mentioned, created four highways endowed with full privilege and inviolability in order to put an end to all dissension and disputes.

The first and greatest of the four highways is called the Fosse Way. It stretches from south to north, starting from a promontory in Cornwall, proceeding by way of Devonshire and Somerset, forth by Tetbury in the

'The first and greatest of the four highways', the Fosse Way as it stretches across Leicestershire

Cotswolds past Coventry to Leicester, and then through desolate levels on to Newark, ending at Lincoln.

The second principal royal highway is called Watling Street. It crosses the Fosse Way diagonally, running from the south-east to the north-west, starting from Dover, proceeding through the middle of Kent, crossing the Thames in London to the west of Westminster. From there it proceeds to St Albans, passing it to the west, and on to Dunstable, Fenny Stratford, Towcester, Weedon Bec, South Lilbourne, and Atherstone on to Gilbert's Hill, now called the Wrekin. From there it follows the Severn past Wroxeter, going on past Stretton, through the middle of Wales to Cardigan and coming to an end at the Irish Sea.

The third highway is called Ermine Street. It extends from the west-north-west to the east-south-east, starting in Menevia, that is, St David's land in West Wales, and extending as far as Southampton. The fourth is called the Icknield Way. It stretches by way of Worcester, Wycombe, Birmingham, Lichfield, Derby, Chesterfield, and York, extending to the mouth of the Tyne.

Chapter Eight

FAMOUS RIVERS AND STREAMS

hree famous rivers run through Britain; by way of them merchants from overseas come by ship to Britain from almost all kinds of nations and countries. These three rivers are the Thames, the Severn and the Humber. The tides ebb and flow at the mouths of these three rivers, and they separate the three regions of the island as if they were three kingdoms. The three regions are Loegria, Cambria and Northumbria, that is, Central England, Wales and Northumbria.

Ranulph observes that the name 'Thames' seems to be one word made up from two river-names belonging to different rivers, namely Thames and Isis; because the River Thames runs through Dorchester and joins the Isis, the whole river from its first source as far as the sea to the east is called 'Tamise' (as in French) or Thames. The Thames begins near Tetbury, three miles to the north of Malmesbury, and originates from a spring that runs east, passing the Fosse Way and dividing Gloucestershire and Wiltshire, drawing with it many other springs and streams. Near Cirencester it becomes large and then goes on towards Bampton, past Oxford, Wallingford, Reading, and London. William of Malmesbury informs us that it runs into the sea in the east near the harbour of Sandwich. It retains its name for forty miles beyond London, and in various places forms a boundary between Kent and Essex and also between Wessex and Mercia. That is a somewhat large proportion of Central England.

Ranulph observes that the Severn is a British river called 'Habren', a British word derived from the name of Estrild's daughter Habren.[1] Because

The River Dee at Chester (see chapter four) which, though not one of the three principal rivers of Britain, was important to Ranulph Higden, who was a monk at Chester

A late medieval map of the Humber estuary giving some indication of its breadth at the river-mouth

The Tower of London, with the White Tower very obviously rendered with a white external wash as was frequent practice with medieval fortified buildings and castles

she was drowned in the river, the Britons called it 'Habren' after her, but the Latin corruption of the name is 'Sabrina', and it is Severn in English. The Severn begins in Central Wales, proceeding eastwards first to Shrewsbury. It then turns south to Bridgnorth, Worcester, and Gloucester, flowing into the sea in the west near Bristol, and separating England and Wales in some places. William of Malmesbury says that the Severn is swift-flowing and full of fish and that the raging, surging, whirling current stirs up and assembles huge piles of gravel. The Severn often rises, overflowing its banks.

Ranulph considers that the Humber takes its name from Humber, King of the Huns, because he was drowned in it; it first flows in an arc from the southern side of York, and subsequently separates the province of Lindsey (which once belonged to the Mercians), from the opposite region, Northumbria. The Trent and the Ouse flow into the Humber, making the river very large. John Trevisa reminds us here that the Mercians were the inhabitants of Central England, as we shall tell you later.

Chapter Nine

ANCIENT CITIES AND TOWNS

n former times, the kingdom of Britain was adorned with twenty-eight noble cities, without taking into account very many walled castles strongly fortified with towers, gates, and bars. Alfred of Beverley tells us that these were the names of the cities: Caerlud, which is London; Caerbranc, which is York; Caerkent, which is Canterbury; Caergorangon, which is Worcester; Caerlirion, which is Leicester; Caerclou, which is Gloucester; Caercolden, which is Colchester; Caerrei, which is Chichester, and which the Saxons used to call Cissancester; Caerceri, which is Cirencester; Caergwent, which is Winchester; Caergrant, which is Cambridge; Caerliel, which is Lugubalia or Carlisle; Caerperis, which is Porchester; Caerdrom, which is Dorchester; Caerludcoit, which is Lincoln, or sometimes Lindecolin; Caermyrthen, which is Merlin's[1] city or Carmarthen; Caersigent, which is Silchester, and is

A woodcut of medieval London from Wynkyn de Worde's 1498 reprint of The Description of Britain

on the Thames not far from Reading, Caerthleon, also known as Caerlegion, formerly Legachester and now Chester; Caerbathon, which is Bath, once known as Achamannus's city,[2] Caerpaladour, which is Septon, nowadays known as Shaftesbury. Ranulph says that other cities are to be found in chronicles interpreting history; we shall now deal with them.

William of Malmesbury describes London as a noble city on the Thames, rich in citizens, wealth, merchants, trade, and commerce. That is the reason why sometimes, when there is a dearth of food in the whole of England, usually the best purchases are to be had in London because of the wholesalers and retailers there. Geoffrey of Monmouth tells us that Brutus (the first King of the Britons) constructed and built this city of London, the first city of Britain, to commemorate the ravaged city of Troy. He called it 'Troyneweth' ('Troy renews itself') and Trinovantum, that is, New Troy. Subsequently King Lud[3] called it Caerlud after himself, to which the Britons took great exception, as Gildas[4] relates. Later the English called the city London, and later still, the Normans called it Loundres; in Latin it is called Londonia.

The Trojan horse, the undoing of the reputed ancestors of the inhabitants of Britain, from a late fifteenth-century illustration of the poet John Lydgate's Troy Book

Rudhudibras, son of King Leil, was the eighth King of the Britons and built Canterbury, the principal city of Kent. He called it Caerkent. Later the English called it Dorobernia, but it is to be distinguished from Dover, which stands on the cliffs of the English Channel; it is twelve English miles from Dover. Subsequently Dorobernia was called Canterbury, and remains so to this day. The same King Rudhudibras built Winchester, calling it Caergwent; the English later called it Wenta and Winchester after a certain bishop there, called Wine, who had all Wessex subject to him. The same king built Paladour, or Septon, now called Shaftesbury. The Britons relate that an eagle once uttered prophecies there.

Bladud, Leil's son, a magician, was the ninth King of the Britons and built Bath, calling it Caerbathon; the English later called it Achamannus's city, but finally it was called Bathonia, that is, Bath. William of Malmesbury tells us how in this city hot baths surge and spring up; people suppose that Julius Caesar[5] constructed such baths there, but Ranulph cites Geoffrey of Monmouth who, in his book about the British, says that Bladud built these baths. Presumably, William of Malmesbury, not having seen that book about

Canterbury, 'the principal city of Kent', as an idealized background to this late fifteenth-century scene of pilgrims departing on horseback, from John Lydgate's Troy Book *in the British Library*

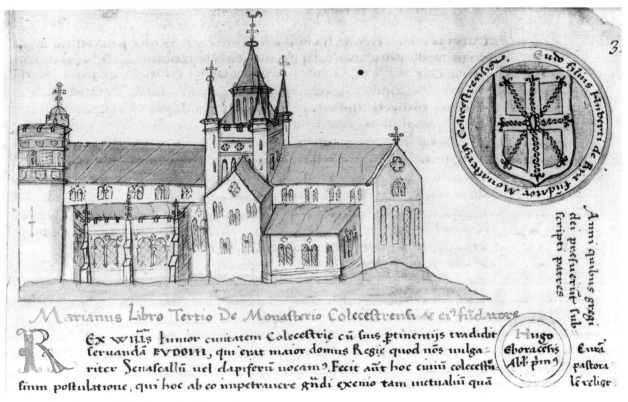

Colchester, from a History of the Abbots of Colchester *of c. 1463*

the British, wrote that on other men's oral authority, or as his own speculation, as he has written other things without due consideration. For these reasons it seems more in accordance with the truth that Bladud did not build the hot baths, nor did Julius Caesar ever perform any such deed. Even if Bladud did construct and build the city, it is much more in keeping with common sense that the water flows through the earth past veins of brimstone and sulphur and so is made hot naturally in its course, springing up in various places in the city, providing hot baths which wash away pus, sores, and scabs. John Trevisa observes: 'If human skill were to construct hot baths lasting for a very long time, this would be consonant with both reason and science, which deals with hot springs and baths in various lands. However, the waters of this bath are more turbulent and sour-tasting than others that I have seen at Aachen in Germany and Aix-les-Bains in Savoy, which are as limpid and clear as any cool stream from a spring. I have bathed in them and tried them.'

According to Ranulph, the Emperor Claudius gave his daughter in marriage to Arviragus, the King of the Britons. It was the same Claudius who built Gloucester for the marriage of his daughter. The Britons first named it after Claudius, but later it was renamed Gloucester after a certain Glora, who was a duke of that region. It stands by the Severn, on the border between England and Wales, as does Shrewsbury, which is set on the top of a hill. Shrewsbury derives its name from the shrubs and fruit-trees which once grew there on the hill. Formerly the Britons called it Pengwern, signifying 'the top of a fir-tree'. Shrewsbury was once the capital of Powys, which extends across Central Wales as far as the Irish Sea.

Nottingham stands on the Trent and was formerly called 'Snottingham', that is, 'a habitation with caves', because the Danes once inhabited it and dug hollows and caves beneath the hard rocks and stones in which to live. Lincoln is the capital of the province of Lindsey and was formerly known as Caerludcoit and later Lindecolin. It is uncertain who first built this city,

Cave-like excavations in Nottinghamshire; despite what The Description of Britain *says, they probably have very little to do with the Danes*

unless it was King Lud, for so it would appear from the name's meaning, for 'caer' is British, meaning 'a city', and 'coit' means 'a wood', and so it seems that Caerludcoit means 'Lud's-wood-town'. King Leir was the son of Bladud and built Leicester on the River Soar and the royal highway, the Fosse Way.

William of Malmesbury tells us that York is a great city on both sides of the River Ouse. It looked as beautiful as Rome until King William the Conqueror destroyed it and the surrounding countryside with fire and flame, so that a pilgrim seeing it now would weep if he had known it in former days. Geoffrey of Monmouth says that Ebrancus, the fifth King of the Britons, built York and named it Caerbranc after himself. He also built two other noble cities, one in Scotland, namely Edinburgh, and another near Scotland, on the borders of England, called Alcluid. Again, Ranulph informs us that Edinburgh is a city in the land of the Picts between the River Tweed and the Scottish sea. It was once known as 'The Castle of Maidens' and was later

Edinburgh, Caxton's 'Castle of Maidens', showing the imposing fortification of Edinburgh Castle

York and its famous Minster; its surviving later medieval splendour shows clearly that the city recovered from the reported destruction by William the Conqueror

called Edinburgh after Edan, King of the Picts, who reigned there in the time of King Egfrith of Northumbria.

Alcluid was once a noble city, though it is now almost unknown to all Englishmen, for under the Britons and Picts it was a splendid city until the coming of the Danes. Afterwards, however, in about the year 870, it was destroyed when the Danes laid waste the countryside of Northumbria. Various authorities give different accounts of where in Britain the city of Alcluid stood. Bede says that it was built to the west of the inlet of the sea which once formed the boundary between the Britons and the Picts; Severus's famous wall[6] comes to an end in the west, and so it appears from Bede's account that it is not far from Carlisle, because that city is located at the end of the wall. Other historians write that the city of Alcluid is the one now known as Aldborough, meaning 'an old town', and that it stands on the

River Ouse not far from Boroughbridge, fifteen miles to the west of York. This appears to be supported by Geoffrey of Monmouth in his book about the deeds of the Britons, where he writes that Elidurus,[7] King of the Britons, was staying in the city of Alcluid for relaxation and hunting, when he came upon his brother Archgalon wandering in a nearby wood called Calateri. However, the wood of Calateri, which is 'Caltrees' in English, reaches almost to York and extends northwards for twenty miles to Aldborough. Most of this wood has now been levelled and the land is cultivated. Yet others would be inclined to believe that Alcluid was the city now known as Burgham, which stands on the River Eden in the northern region of Westmorland, on the borders of Cumberland. Splendid traces of it are still to be seen. Now, make up your own minds where it stands! John Trevisa comments: 'It is not hard to find a solution if one notes that many towns are known by the same name, like Carthage in Africa and Cartagena in Spain, or Newport in Wales and Newport in the parish of Berkeley, or again, Wootton-under-Edge and Wootton Bassett, or yet again, Wickwar, Wickpain, and Wick in the parish of Berkeley. Furthermore, two principal towns of shires are both called Hampton, namely Southampton and Northampton, so it appears from historical accounts that there was one Alcluid in Yorkshire and another in Westmorland; one was on the edge of the right bank of the western inlet separating England and Scotland. Yet, as Bede says, Alcluid was a very mighty city, standing right beside a river called the Cluid; there is no such river in either Yorkshire or Westmorland, as the local people tell me. Some people say that the River Cluid is now called the Sulwach, which is only five miles distant from Carlisle.

Carlisle itself is a city to the north-west of the northern region of England. It has another name, Lugubal, and it was built by Leil, the seventh King of the Britons. Ranulph says that in this city there is part of the famous wall which runs across Northumbria. William of Malmesbury relates that in Carlisle there is still a three-chambered building, constructed of vaulting-stones, which could never be destroyed either by storms or by fire. Also, in the countryside close by in Westmorland, on the front of a three-chambered dwelling there is an inscription as follows: *Marii victoriae*. I am in some doubt as to what this inscription signifies, unless it were the case that some of the tribe of the Cumbri once lodged there after the consul Marius had expelled them from Italy, but it rather seems that it is written to commemorate Marius, the King of the Britons and son of Arviragus.[8] According to Geoffrey of Monmouth's book about the Britons (which William of Malmesbury never saw), this Marius defeated Roderick, King of the Picts there.

At the church of Hagustald or Hexham there is a ruined site eighty miles north-west of York; according to William of Malmesbury it is more or less derelict. It once belonged to the see of York, and formerly had arches and vaults in the Roman style. Now the place is called both Hestoldesham and Heglesham. Bede says that the site is right beside the long wall constructed by the Romans in the north.

Ranulph comments that there is a difference between the province of 'Lindefar' and the church of Lindisfarne; the province of 'Lindefar' is identical with Lindsey, lying to the east of Lincoln, its principal city, whose

'The long wall constructed by the Romans in the north': Hadrian's Wall in stern splendour at Borcovicium, Northumberland

Bamburgh Castle in Northumberland; the threatening skyscape emphasizes the massive strength of the fortification

first bishop was Sexwulf, according to Bede. However, Bede says that the church of Lindisfarne is on an island called Holy Island in the River Tweed near Berwick, and from Bede's observations we gather that the Tweed runs into the famous inlet of the sea now dividing the English from the Scots on the east side. In that inlet there are three islands: one being known as Mailros and now Meuros; then over towards the west there is Lindisfarne church on Holy Island; the third is further on still and is called Farne Island, or Farny Island. Two miles further up from this island is a royal city on the banks of the Tweed which was once called Bebbanburgh (that is, 'Bebba's city') and is now known as Bamburgh. It has a very strong castle.

According to Gerald of Wales in his 'Journey', there are two cities called both Caerlegion and Caerleon. One is in Demetia in South Wales, also known as Caerusk, where the River Usk flows into the Severn close to Glamorgan. Long ago, Belinus, King of the Britons, built the city, which was formerly the principal city of Demetia in South Wales. Later, in the time of the Emperor Claudius, it was called 'The City of Legions' when, at the request of Queen Genuissa,[9] Vespasian and Arviragus established a treaty and Roman legions were sent to Ireland. At that time Caerleon was a noble city of very high standing, splendidly built by the Romans and surrounded by walls of baked brick. The great splendour which existed there in former times is still visible in many places, for example: the huge palaces; a giant's tower; fine baths; remains of temples; and sites of theatres, which were lofty and noble enclosures for sitting and standing in and for viewing displays. Such places were splendidly enclosed by noble walls which, to some extent, still stand and almost form an enclosure. Both inside and outside the walls there remains much subterranean construction, such as water-pipes, corridors beneath the ground, and baths. You can also see air-ducts, marvellously constructed and narrowly enclosed, which conduct warm air in a wonderful fashion.

In this city of Caerleon there were once three splendid churches: one dedicated to Saint Julius the Martyr amidst a great company of virgins; the second, very richly adorned, dedicated to Saint Aaron,[10] belonging to the order of the Black Canons; and the third, the principal mother church of

Wales and its chief see. Later, however, the principal see was transferred from this city to Menevia, Saint David's land in West Wales. Saint Amphibalus, who taught Saint Alban,[11] was born in Caerleon. The messengers from Rome came to the great King Arthur there, if it is permissible to believe that. John Trevisa observes that if Gerald of Wales was doubtful whether or not it was permissible to believe this, it was scarcely a prudent course to record it in his books, for as some people would point out, it is a remarkable delusion to write a long history to record things permanently for posterity, whilst still remaining uncertain whether one's belief is misplaced. If all his books were of this nature, what would they contain worthy of the name of instruction; especially since he cites no proof for either view, for he does not reveal what prompts him to say what he does?

Ranulph reminds us that there is another City of Legions where his chronicle was produced, as is clearly manifest from the first chapter of his first book. (John Trevisa reminds us that this refers to the Latin *Polychronicon*; Ranulph, who wrote that, did not translate it into English, nor did Trevisa translate it into English in the place where it was first compiled in Latin. The declaration of the man who produced the *Polychronicon* is inscribed thus at its opening: *presentem cronicam compilavit frater Ranulphus Cestrensis monachus*, which in English is: 'Brother Ranulph, a monk of Chester, compiled and produced this present chronicle.' Ranulph indicates that the City of Legions, also known as Chester, stands at the borders of England close to Wales, between two tidal estuaries; those of the Dee and the Mersey. In the time of the Britons this city was the capital of the whole of Venedocia, that is, North Wales. Its founder is unknown; anyone looking at the foundations of its huge stones would rather think that it was the work of Romans or giants than that it was constructed by the Britons. This city was formerly called Caerthleon in the British language and Legecestria in Latin; in English it is both Chester and the City of Legions, because the legions of knights despatched by Julius Caesar to conquer Ireland overwintered there, and later the Emperor Claudius sent legions from Chester to conquer the Orkneys. Despite what William of Malmesbury dreamed up from other men's accounts about this city, it has an abundance of provisions, grain, meat, fish, and especially fine salmon. Much merchandise comes into and goes out of Chester. Nearby there are salt springs, metals, and mineral ores. The Northumbrians once destroyed Chester, but later Ethelfleda, Lady of the Mercians, rebuilt it and made it much larger. In this city there are subterranean passageways with marvellously constructed vaults and stonework, three-chambered buildings and huge stones inscribed with the names of men of old. The names of Julius Caesar and other eminent men are incised amongst surrounding inscriptions. This is the city that was destroyed by Ethelfrith, King of Northumbria, who killed almost two thousand monks from the monastery of Bangor in its neighbourhood. It is to this city that King Edgar once came with seven of his under-kings. A certain poet breaks out into verse in praise of this city in the following manner:

> Chester, or as one might say 'Castle-town', takes its name from a castle. The identity of its founder is now lost. Once Legecestria, it is now called the City of Legions. Both the Welsh and the English now hold it in high honour. All the stones of its walls seem like the work of Hercules. That pile of masonry is set to endure in its might for long ages. The small stones of the Saxons are set directly on top of the huge ones. A double vault is to be found there concealed under the ground. With its fine tilth Chester helps many people of the western region. This city is abundantly provided with fish, meat and grain. Godescalle,[12] a former emperor, lies there, as does King Henry the Fourth; the earth is a fit abode for them. The dust of King Harold[13] is preserved there. Bacchus and Mercury, Mars and Venus, Laverna Proteus and Pluto hold sway in the city.

John Trevisa comments on these lines: 'God knows what this is supposed to mean; yet poets in their peculiar way of expressing themselves pretend that each kind of skill and activity has its own individual god. Hence they imagined a god of battle and fighting, and named him Mars. Then they imagined a god of covetousness of wealth and merchandise and called him Mercury. Likewise, Bacchus was designated god of wine, Venus goddess of love and beauty, Laverna god of theft and robbery, Proteus god of falsehood and dissembling, and Pluto god of Hell. And so it appears that these verses are intended to mean that the gods mentioned hold sway and are honoured in Chester: Mars with fighting and brawling, Mercury with covetousness of wealth and merchandise; Bacchus with heavy drinking; Venus with lustful amorousness; Laverna with theft and robbery; and Proteus with falsehood and guile. Indeed, Pluto, god of Hell, does not remain without votaries.' Ranulph had already observed that wherever the ways of Babylon increase their sway, they make all the more noise about it.

Chapter Ten

PROVINCES AND SHIRES

ote that England contains thirty-two shires and provinces (now known as earldoms), not counting Cornwall and the islands. Alfred of Beverley gives the following names of the earldoms and shires: Kent, Sussex, Surrey, Hampshire, Berkshire (deriving its name from a bare oak in the forest of Windsor, since men of the shire were accustomed to gather and make agreements, and hold consultations and discussions there), Wiltshire (once known as the province of Semeran), Somerset, Dorset and Devonshire (now called Devonia in Latin). These nine southern shires are divided by the Thames from the rest of England and were formerly governed and ruled by West Saxon law. The list continues: Essex, Middlesex, Suffolk, Norfolk, Hertfordshire, Huntingdonshire, Northamptonshire, Cambridgeshire, Bedfordshire, Buckinghamshire, Leicestershire, Derbyshire, Nottinghamshire, Lincolnshire, Yorkshire, Durham, Northumberland, Carlisleshire with Cumberland, Applebyshire with Westmorland, and Lancashire (containing five smaller shires). These fifteen northern and eastern shires were once governed and ruled by the law called the Danelaw;[1] but Oxfordshire, Warwickshire, Gloucestershire, Worcestershire, Herefordshire, Shropshire, Staffordshire, Cheshire, the central and western shires, were formerly governed by the law known as

A coin bearing a portrait of King Alfred the Great (d. 899), noted in this work as an eminent lawgiver

Mercian from the Latin name, and in English as 'Merchenelaw'.

Note that Yorkshire stretches only from the River Humber to the River Tees, and yet in Yorkshire there are twenty-two hundreds ('hundred' and 'candred' are the same thing; 'candred' is a word derived from Welsh and Irish, signifying a region containing a hundred towns; in English it is also called 'wapentake', because formerly, at the coming of a new lord, tenants were accustomed to yield up their weapons to pay homage). Durham stretches from the River Tees to the River Tyne. And to speak of Northumberland itself: it stretches from the River Tyne to the River Tweed, the border of Scotland. Then if the region of Northumbria, which once stretched from the Humber to the Tweed, should now be reckoned as one shire and earldom, as it was in days gone by, there are only thirty-two shires in England; but if Northumbria is divided into six shires: Yorkshire, Durham, Northumberland, Carlisleshire, Applebyshire, and Lancashire; there are thirty-six shires in England, not including Cornwall or the islands. King William the Conqueror had all these provinces and shires surveyed and measured; in his time there were to be found thirty-six-and-a-half shires, fifty-two thousand and eighty towns, forty-five thousand and two parish churches, sixty thousand and fifteen knights' fiefs,[2] of which men in orders possessed twenty-eight thousand and fifteen fiefs. Nowadays, however,

Britain as it was in Caxton's day

woodlands have been cut down and the land has been newly tilled and much increased from what existed at that time, and many towns and villages have been built; so there are many more villages and towns than there were then. Moreover, though Alfred of Beverley has said previously that Cornwall is not classified amongst the shires of England, it is quite proper to classify it amongst them, because it belongs neither to Wales nor to Scotland but is in England, adjoining Devonshire. Therefore in England there can be reckoned to be thirty-seven-and-a-half shires, adding it to the rest.

Chapter Eleven

LAWS AND THEIR NAMES

 unwallo, also called Moliuncius, enacted the first laws in Britain. They were known as Moliuncius's laws, and were solemnly observed until William the Conqueror's time. Amongst his laws, he ordained that cities, temples, and roads leading to them, and farmers' ploughs, should have the privilege and power to offer sanctuary to all men fleeing to them for help and refuge. Later Marcia, Queen of the Britons and wife of Guitelinus,[1] from whom some people think the province of Mercia took its name, enacted a very just, sensible, and fair law which was known as 'Merchenelaga'; the law of the Mercians. Gildas, author of historical works about the Britons, translated these two laws from the British language into Latin, and later, King Alfred[2] translated them all from Latin into Anglo-Saxon, in which they were called 'Merchenelaw'. The same King Alfred also wrote it in English, and added another law called West Saxon law. Then afterwards the Danes became rulers in this country, thus giving rise to the third law, called Danelaw.

From these three laws King Edward the Confessor produced a single common law which is still called Saint Edward's Law. I consider it a useful task to record and explain here many terms from these laws, such as: *myndebruche*, meaning injury to honour and good name, or in French, *bleschur d'honnour*; *burbrucg*,[3] in French *bleschur de court ou de cloys*; *grithbruch*, breach of

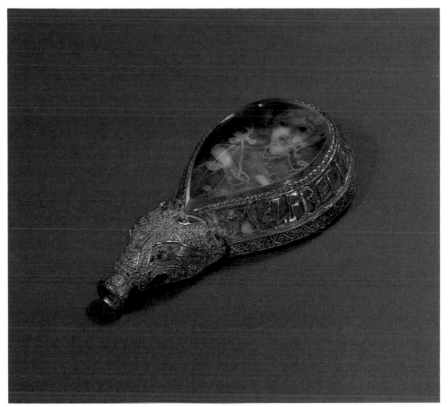

The Alfred Jewel, bearing the royal portrait with the inscription 'Alfred ordered me to be made' in Anglo-Saxon, now in the Ashmolean Museum, Oxford

the peace; *myskennyng*, variation of testimony in court; *schewyng*, displaying merchandise, or in French, *disploier de merchandyse*; *hamsoken* or *hamfare*, an affray conducted in a house; *forstallyng*, injury or hindrance perpetrated on the King's highway; *frithsoken*,[4] in French, *surete en defense*; *sake*, a forfeit; *soke*, a lawsuit, from which comes *soken*; *theam*, a bondman's suit; *fyghtyngwyte*, the penalty for fighting; *blodewyte*, reparation for bloodshed; *flitwyte*, reparation for quarrelling; *leirwyte*, reparation for having intercourse with a bondswoman; *gultwite*, amends for an offence; *scot*, a tax payable in labour supervised by the bailiffs; *hidage* or *taillage*, a tax on the number of hides of land; *Danegeld*, a tax paid to the Danes, namely threepence for every *bovata terrae* or amount of land allotted to an ox; a *wapentake* is the same thing as a hundred, since the area of a hundred towns used to render weapons as homage to an incoming lord; *lostage*, a customary exaction at markets and fairs; and *stallage*, a customary exaction for a place in the street during a fair.

Chapter Twelve

BRITAIN'S KINGDOMS AND THEIR
BOUNDARIES AND LIMITS

he kingdom of Britain remained undivided as a single kingdom for the Britons from the time of the firstcomer Brutus until that of Julius Caesar. From then until Severus's[1] time this land was a tributary of the Romans. Nonetheless, they had kings here in this island from Severus up to the last prince, Gratian. At this point the British succession failed, and so the Romans reigned in Britain. Later they ceased to reign in this country because it was far from Rome and because of the considerable trouble they had in other areas. Then the Scots and Picts, led astray by Maximus the tyrant, attacked and made war on Britain with a great force of men of arms for a long time, until the Saxons came at the request of the Britons to fight the Picts, and expelled Gurmund, the Irish king, with his Picts, and the Britons as well, along with their king, called Careticus. Hence the Saxons were the victors, and every province created a king for itself, according to its strength. Afterwards, however, these seven kingdoms in succession were all united into one single

A portrait of Julius Caesar on a Roman denarius in the British Museum

A portrait on a coin of King Egbert of Wessex, who added Essex to his royal possessions

The martyrdom of King Edmund of East Anglia by the Danes, shot to death by many arrows like St Sebastian, from a manuscript in the British Library

kingdom under Prince Athelstan. Nonetheless, the Danes continued attacking this country from the time of Ethelwulf, King Alfred's father, until that of King Edward the Confessor; that is, for about a hundred and seventy years, with an uninterrupted period of their own rule for thirty years. After this period of Danish rule, King Edward the Confessor ruled for just over twenty-three years, and after him, Harold[2] held the kingdom for nine months. After them, the Normans reigned and have done so up to the present day, but only He to Whom nothing is unknown knows how long they will continue to reign.

Ranulph, whom I follow, at this point declares his intention to give a brief account of the seven kingdoms mentioned previously: of their boundaries, limits and divisions; of when they began and how long they

The first Hengist, the Germanic war-leader, being destroyed, along with his army, by King Arthur at the Battle of Mount Badon. From a manuscript in the British Library

King Edward the Confessor, portrayed in stained glass in the great west window of Canterbury Cathedral

lasted. Alfred of Beverley relates that the first kingdom was that of Kent, stretching from the south Ocean (the sea surrounding the world), to the River Thames. The first Hengist ruled there, beginning, according to the reckoning of Dionysius,[3] in the year of Our Lord 455. That kingdom lasted three hundred and sixty-eight years under fifteen kings until the deposition of Baldred,[4] when Egbert, King of Wessex, united the kingdom with his own. The second kingdom was that of Sussex, which had Kent on its east side, the sea and the Isle of Wight to the south, Hampshire to the west and Surrey to the north. Aelle[5] first ruled there with his three sons, beginning his reign thirty years after the coming of the Angles. The kingdom of Sussex, however, was subsumed within a few years by other kingdoms. The third kingdom was that of Essex, which had the sea to the east, the region of London to the west, the Thames to the south, and Suffolk to the north. There were ten kings of Essex from the first Sebert's time to the coming of the Danes, and they were to some extent subject to other kings. For the most part, however, they were subject to the Kings of Mercia until Egbert, King of Wessex, united Essex with his own kingdom. The fourth kingdom was that of East Anglia; containing Norfolk and Suffolk, with the sea to the east and the north, Cambridgeshire to the north-west, Saint Edmund's dyke and Hertfordshire to the west and Essex to the south. This kingdom lasted under twelve kings until the time when King Edmund was killed and the Danes wrongfully appropriated the kingdoms of both East Anglia and Essex. Afterwards the Danes were driven out or subjugated. King Edward the Elder united both these kingdoms to his own, Wessex, which was the fifth kingdom and lasted longest of them all. To the south it had Sussex, to the north the Thames and to the south and west, it had Ocean, the world-sea. In it reigned Cerdic with his son Cynric, beginning to reign in the year of Our Lord 519, seventy-one years after the coming of the Angles, according to Dionysius. The other kingdoms were subsumed by this kingdom. The sixth kingdom was of Mercia and was the largest of all. Its boundaries and limits were: the River Dee at Chester and the Severn at Shrewsbury as far as Bristol in the west; the North Sea in the east; the Thames as far as London in the south; and the River Humber, progressing westwards and downwards to the River Mersey where it flows into the sea by the Wirral peninsula in the north. According to Dionysius, Penda, the son of Wibba, first reigned in this kingdom in the year of Our Lord 626.

Chapter Thirteen

BISHOPRICS AND SEES

ucius was the first Christian King of the Britons. In his time there were three archiepiscopal sees in Britain: one at London; the second at York; and the third at Caerleon-on-Usk, formerly the City of Legions in Glamorgan. Twenty-eight bishops, called *flamines*, were subject to these archiepiscopal sees. Cornwall and all Central England as far as the Humber were subject to the see of London; all Northumbria from the curve of the Humber, and the whole of Scotland to York; and the whole of Wales to Caerleon.

There were formerly seven bishops in Wales, but now there are only

The ancient church of St Martin in Canterbury, perhaps our earliest Christian site

King Arthur arriving at Caerleon in Wales, from an illustrated mid-fourteenth century version of The Brut, *a versified history of Britain, now in the British Library*

four. At that time the Severn formed the boundary between England and Wales. William of Malmesbury relates that in the time of the Saxons, although Saint Gregory had granted London the privilege of being the archbishop's see, Saint Augustine (who had been sent to England by Saint Gregory), notwithstanding that, transferred the archiepiscopal see from London to Canterbury after Saint Gregory's time, at the request of King Ethelbert and the citizens and burgesses of Canterbury. There it has remained until the present day, except that during an intervening period King Offa of Mercia was angry with the people of Canterbury and deprived them of the privileges. He honoured Adulf, Bishop of Lichfield, with the archbishop's pallium[1] with the formal approval of Pope Hadrian (obtained by the sending of gifts). Nevertheless, under King Cenwulf it was restored to Canterbury.

The eminence of York has always lasted there and still remains, even though Scotland has been withdrawn from its jurisdiction with the passing of time. According to Gerald's 'Journey', the archiepiscopal see was transferred in Saint David's time[2] from Caerleon to Menevia in western Demetia by the Irish Sea, under King Arthur. From the time of Saint David to that of Archbishop Sampson there were twenty-three archbishops in Menevia. At the time of Archbishop Sampson, an epidemic of the yellow sickness, or jaundice, struck the whole of Wales. Then the Archbishop took the pallium with him and went to the Breton region, Armorica, or 'Little Britain', where he was bishop of Dolensis. From that time until the days of King Henry the First of England, there were in Menevia (or St Davids) twenty-one bishops completely devoid of the pallium, either from folly or from poverty. Nevertheless, after that time the bishops of Wales were consecrated by the bishop of Menevia or St Davids, and he in turn was consecrated by the bishops of Wales as his own suffragans, offering no profession or submission to any other church. Other bishops coming afterwards were consecrated at Canterbury at the command and behest of the king. To symbolize that consecration and subjection, Boniface, Archbishop of Canterbury and Papal Legate, sang a solemn mass in every cathedral church in Wales. He was the first Archbishop of Canterbury to do so in Wales and it was accomplished in

R eis Auelberd ge kent teueit
D e linage Hengist eu esteit
C il ad seint Austin baptisez
E en le seint fonuce regenerez

Q upres le reis sit la meisme
R egeuerey z baptize
P ar la terre aloue sarmonaue
M asters sesaut clers ordemaue
B uit li Reis z li sarsou
P runies li englesh z li barou
M eut uiz receuz baptesine
E nfauz teuez et oiut de creme
A reis sey est repaire
M it esteit iorouse z lie
L apostoill ad toe ote
C om oiut le peple regenere
S ackballem en gentil bier

The baptism of King Ethelbert of Kent by St Augustine, from the same mid-fourteenth-century manuscript of The Brut

the time of King Henry the Second.

Ranulph observes that now there are only two Primates in all England: those of Canterbury and York. Thirteen bishops in England and four in Wales are subject to the Primate of Canterbury. The Primate of York has only two suffragans in England: the bishops of Carlisle and Durham. I shall now describe all these sees and the changes in their location in the following section.

Note that at the beginning of Holy Church in England, bishops ordained their sees in lowly, simple places suitable for contemplation, prayers, and devotion, but in the time of William the Conqueror it was proclaimed by decree of canon law that bishops should come out from small towns into great cities. For this reason the see of Dorchester was transferred to Lincoln, that of Lichfield to Chester, that of Thetford to Norwich, that of Sherborne to Salisbury, that of Wells to Bath, that of Cornwall to Exeter, and that of Selsey to Chichester. The Bishop of Rochester has no parish, but he is the chaplain of the Archbishop of Canterbury. Since the see of Canterbury was first ordained by Saint Augustine it has never been removed. Chichester has subject to it only Sussex and the Isle of Wight; the see was formerly located at Selsey in the time of Archbishop Theodore,[3] and lasted there for a hundred and thirty-three years under twenty bishops, the first being Wilfred, and the last, Stigand, who transferred the see from Selsey to Chichester at William the Conqueror's command.

The Bishops of the Western Regions

William of Malmesbury reminds us that the whole province of Wessex has always had one bishop from its beginnings until the time of Theodore. By the grant of King Cynegils[4] of Wessex, Birinus, the first bishop, established a see at Dorchester, a humble place to the south of Oxford, near Wallingford, at the confluence of the Thames with another river. After Birinus's death, King Cenwalh[5] established a see at Winchester as his father had intended. There, Agilbert (a Frenchman) was the first bishop of the whole province of Wessex.

The crossing of Wells Cathedral, showing the splendid arches added in 1338 to support the tower

Dorchester Abbey, Oxfordshire, a former episcopal see, where Bishop Birinus first held sway

From that time the city and the see of Dorchester belonged to the province of Mercia, because it stands on the Thames, which separates Mercia and Wessex. After Agilbert was expelled from Winchester (then called Winton), an English bishop called Wine ruled there, from whom some people consider that the city derived its name Winchester, apparently meaning 'Wine's city'. In the end he was expelled too, being succeeded by Leutherius,[6] nephew of the same Agilbert. After Leutherius, Hedda was Bishop there for a time. After his death, Archbishop Theodore established two bishops for the province of Wessex: Daniel at Winchester, in whose control were two regions, Surrey and Hampshire; and Aldhelm at Sherborne, in whose control were six regions, Berkshire, Wiltshire, Somerset, Dorset, Devonshire, and Cornwall. John Trevisa concludes from this that Wessex contained Surrey, Hampshire, Berkshire, Wiltshire, Somerset, Dorset, Devonshire, and Cornwall. William of Malmesbury relates that afterwards, in the time of King Edward the Elder,[7] three others were established by command of Pope Formosus in addition to these two sees: at Wells for Somerset; at Crediton for Devonshire; and at St Germans for Cornwall. Not very long afterwards the sixth see was finally established at Ramsbury for Wiltshire. Finally, at the command of King William the Conqueror, all these sees except Winchester were removed from small towns to great cities; Sherborne and Ramsbury being transferred to Salisbury, to which Berkshire, Wiltshire, and Dorset are now subject. The see of Wells transferred to Bath, and the whole of Somerset is now subject to it. The sees of Crediton and of Cornwall were transferred to Exeter, to which Devon and Cornwall are now subject.

The Eastern Bishops

It is well known that the East Saxons have always been subject to the Bishop of London from the earliest beginnings to the present day. However, the province of East Anglia (containing Norfolk and Suffolk) had one bishop at Dunwich. He was called Felix, a Burgundian, and was bishop there for seventeen years. After him Thomas was bishop for five years, succeeded by

The episcopal seal of Bishop Æthelwald of Dunwich

Boniface for seventeen years. Then afterwards Bisi was ordained by Theodore and ruled the province alone for as long as he retained his health. After him, until the time of King Egbert of Wessex, there were two bishops in charge of the province for a hundred and forty-three years: one at Dunwich and one at Elmham. Nevertheless, after the time of King Ludecans of Mercia, there was only one see left, at Elmham. This was until the fifth year of the reign of William the Conqueror, when Herfastus, the twenty-third bishop of the eastern region, transferred the see to Thetford, and his successor Herbert transferred the see from Thetford to Norwich with King William Rufus's[8] permission. King Henry the First[9] established the nearby see of Ely in the ninth year of his reign, putting Cambridgeshire (which had previously been part of the diocese of Lincoln) under its control. To compensate for its removal he granted the Bishop of Lincoln a fine town called Spalding.

The south side of the ambulatory of Norwich Cathedral, with unusually graceful Norman arch-work

The splendidly Celtic-geometrical Lichfield Gospels (720–30), often called St Chad's Gospels, showing the lion symbolizing St Mark, and the opening page of his gospel

The Bishops of Mercia

William of Malmesbury asks us to note that since the kingdom of Mercia has always been the largest, it was therefore divided into more bishoprics, especially by the instigation of King Offa, who was King of Mercia for forty years. He transferred the archiepiscopal see from Canterbury to Lichfield with the consent of Pope Hadrian. The province of Mercia and Lindsey had a single bishop at Lichfield during its first reception of Christianity in the time of King Wulfran. The first bishop there was called Dwina, the second Celath, and both were Scots. After them came the third, Trumphere. The fourth was called Jarumannus, and the fifth, Chad. However, in the time of Wulfhere's brother Ethelfred, after Chad's death, Archbishop Theodore ordained Wynfrith, Chad's deacon, as bishop. Despite that, he subsequently dethroned him because he was disobedient in a certain matter, and ordained Sexwulf, abbot of Medehamstede (now Peterborough) in his stead. Yet after Sexwulf's fourth year, Archbishop Theodore ordained five bishops in the province of Mercia: Bosel to Worcester; Cuthwine to Lichfield; Sexwulf himself to Chester; and Ethelwine to Lindsey, in the city of Sidenia. He also took Eata, a monk of the abbey of Saint Hilda at Whitby, and made him

Bishop of Dorchester (then known as Dorking) near Oxford. In this way its see, which had belonged to Wessex in Bishop Birinus's time, belonged to Mercia from Archbishop Theodore's time.

King Ethelred of Mercia had devastated Kent, and Bishop Sexwulf took Bishop Pictas of Rochester from Kent and made him the first Bishop of Hereford. When Sexwulf finally died, Hedda succeeded him as Bishop of Lichfield and Wilfred, driven out of Northumbria, became Bishop of Chester. However, after two years, King Aldfrith of Northumbria died and Wilfred returned to his own see of Hexham. So, Hedda held both bishoprics: Lichfield and Chester. He was succeeded by Albinus, also known as Wor, after whom came bishops Torta of Chester and Witta of Lichfield, whilst Eata still remained at Dorchester. After his death the bishops of Lindsey held his see for a hundred and fifty-four years until Remigius transferred the see to Lincoln with the assent of King William the Conqueror. In Edgar's[10] reign, however, Bishop Leofwine united the two sees of Chester and Lindsey for the duration of his lifetime.

The Bishops of Northumbria

William of Malmesbury tells us that there was one see at York for the whole province of Northumbria. Paulinus[11] was the first to hold the see, being ordained by the Bishop of Canterbury. He held the see of York for seven years. Afterwards, when King Edwin had been killed and things were in turmoil, Paulinus departed, travelling by sea to Kent and taking the pallium with him. Thus the bishopric of York ceased to exist for thirty years, and the use of the pallium was suspended there for a hundred and twenty-five years until Bishop Egbert, brother of the King of Northumbria, restored it on the Pope's authority. Ranulph tells us that in the reign of Saint Oswald,[12] Aidan (a Scot) was bishop in Bernicia, the northern part of Northumbria, followed by Finan and then Colman. He finally departed to Scotland in high dudgeon because Wilfred rebuked him for celebrating Easter Day[13] contrary to the laws of the Church. Thirty years after Paulinus's departure, Wilfred was

A silver plaque, depicting a bishop wearing his pallium and holding a book, from Hexham

made Bishop of York. However, Bede says that whilst he was staying for a long time in France on matters connected with his consecration, Chad was removed from his abbey of Lastingham and wrongfully placed in the see of York with the assent of King Oswy. Three years later, however, Archbishop Theodore removed him, assigning him to the province of Mercia, and restored Wilfred to the see of York. Yet Wilfred was subsequently removed from his see, because of a quarrel which had arisen between him and King Egfrith, with the assistance of Archbishop Theodore who had been corrupted by some kind of bribe. This was done after Wilfred has been Bishop of York for ten years. Then, at the King's prompting, Theodore appointed Bosa as Bishop of York, Cuthbert to the church of Hexham, and Eata to the church of Lindisfarne, now called Holy Island, in the River Tweed. Aidan had first founded the see. Theodore appointed Eadhed, who had returned from Lindsey, Bishop of Ripon, an office previously held by Wilfred. Theodore sent Trumwine to the land of the Picts on the border between England and Scotland, to a place called Candida Casa or Whithorn. Saint Ninian, a Briton, had been its first founder and teacher.

All these sees, however, failed as time went on, with the exception of York, and the see of Candida Casa or Galloway, which belonged to England at

St Cuthbert instructing his monks, from a twelfth-century illustrated manuscript of Bede's Life of Cuthbert *probably made in Durham*

Durham Cathedral dominating the river

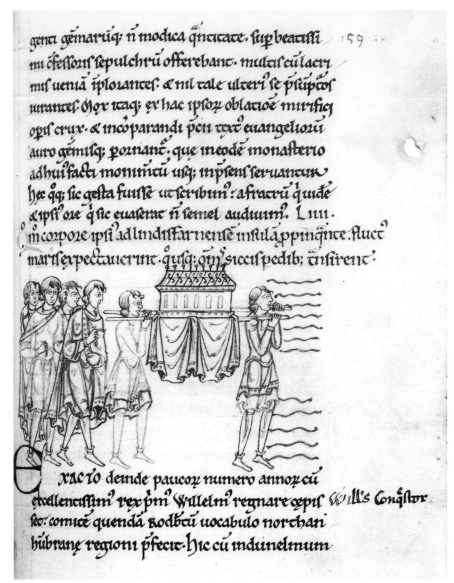

The coffin of St Cuthbert being carried back across the sands to Holy Island, from a manuscript in the Bodleian Library, Oxford

that time, lasting for many years under ten bishops, until it became powerless because of the destruction wrought by the Picts. The sees of Hexham and Lindisfarne were at one time united under nine bishops for about ninety years and lasted until the coming of the Danes. At that time under the sway of Hinguar and Hubba, Bishop Ardulf travelled around for a long time with Saint Cuthbert's[14] body until the time of King Alfred of Wessex, and the see of Lindisfarne was located at Kunegestre, also called Kingsborough, and now known as Ubbeford-on-Tweed. In the end, in the seventeenth year of the reign of King Egbert (son of King Edgar), the see was transferred to Durham, and Saint Cuthbert's body was taken there at the instigation of Bishop

Edmund. From that time the sees of Hexham and Lindisfarne completely ceased to exist. King Henry the First created a new see at Carlisle in the ninth year of his reign.

The Archbishops

The Archbishop of Canterbury has authority over thirteen bishops in England and four in Wales: Rochester, which has only Kent under its control; London, subject to which are Essex, Middlesex and half of Hertfordshire; Chichester, which has charge of Sussex and the Isle of Wight; Winchester, with Hampshire and Surrey in its control; Salisbury, subject to which are Berkshire, Wiltshire and Dorset; Exeter, which has charge of Devon and Cornwall; Bath, ruling Somerset alone; Worcester, administering Gloucestershire, Worcestershire and half of Warwickshire; Hereford, subject to which are Herefordshire and part of Shropshire; Chester, which subsumes Coventry and Lichfield and controls Cheshire, Staffordshire, Derbyshire, half of Warwickshire, part of Shropshire and part of Lancashire from the Mersey to the River Ribble; Lincoln, subject to which are the provinces between the Thames and the Humber, namely Lincolnshire, Leicestershire, Northamptonshire, Huntingdonshire, Bedfordshire, Buckinghamshire, Oxfordshire and half of Hertfordshire; Ely, controlling Cambridgeshire with the exception of Merlond; and Norwich, which has charge of Merlond, Norfolk, and Suffolk. In addition, the Archbishop of Canterbury has four suffragans in Wales, namely Llandaff, St Davids, Bangor, and St Asaph. The Archbishop of York now has charge of only two bishops, those of Durham and Carlisle. As Ranulph observes, there are thus only two primates in England. Their relative positions, and the respects in which one of them must obey and be subject to the other, will be fully explained.

In about the year of Our Lord 1072, in the presence of King William and the English bishops, the issues between these two primates were investigated and dealt with at the Pope's command. It was decreed and pronounced that the Primate of York must be subordinate to the Primate of Canterbury in matters pertaining to the worship of God and the faith of Holy Church, so that wherever in England the Primate of Canterbury may wish to summon and command a council of clergy to convene, the Primate of York is obliged to attend with his suffragans and to obey the decree made in due accordance with the laws of the Church. On the death of the Primate of Canterbury, the Primate of York must come to Canterbury and with the other bishops he must consecrate the elected successor; thus consecrating his own superior. On the death of the Primate of York, his successor must go to the Primate of Canterbury and be consecrated by him, offering his profession and oath of obedience according to the laws of the Church. In about the year of Our Lord 1195, in the time of King Richard,[15] guidelines were laid down for the rights and duties of each of the primates, with information about their mutual relations, during the times of Thurstan, Thomas, and other Bishops of York from the Conquest until the late King Henry's[16] days, and how they evaded each other's control. As this is simply a summary, not a full account, it would be tedious to relate all the evidence cited there.

Chapter Fourteen

THE NUMBER AND KINDS OF PEOPLE WHO HAVE INHABITED BRITAIN

he Britons first inhabited this island in the eighteenth year of the prophet Eli, or in the eleventh year of Silvius Posthumus, King of Latium, that is, forty-three years after the destruction of Troy and four hundred and thirty-two years before the founding of Rome. Bede tells us that they set out and came here from Armorica or Brittany, now called the second Britain. For a long time they held the southern regions of this country. It happened afterwards in the time of Vespasian, the Roman ruler, that the Picts set sail from Scythia upon Ocean, the sea surrounding the world, and, driven by the wind, they reached the north coast of Ireland, where they found the Scots,[1] from whom they requested land to live in. They were not granted any, because Ireland, as the Scots said, could not support both races. The Scots sent the Picts to the

The Trojan Brutus camping on the banks of the Loire on his way to settle in Britain, from Jean de Warrin's History of England, *c. 1471*

northern extremity of Britain and offered them help against their enemies, the Britons, if they should rise up against them. They took wives from amongst their daughters, on condition that if a dispute arose about who ought to be King, they were to elect him from the maternal rather than from the paternal line; from the women's rather than the men's kin.

Geoffrey of Monmouth relates that in the time of the Emperor Vespasian, when Marius, son of Arviragus, was King of the Britons, a certain Roderick came from Scythia and started to lay Scotland waste. King Marius then killed this Roderick and granted the northern region of Scotland, called Caithness, as a dwelling-place for the men who had accompanied Roderick and been vanquished by Marius. These men had no wives, however, and could obtain none from the British nation, so they sailed to Ireland and married Irishmen's daughters, on the condition that descent on the mother's side should take precedence in questions of inheritance and succession. However, Gerald of Wales tells us that in Servius's commentary on Virgil, it is said that the Picts are actually the Agathyrsi who used to inhabit the Scythian marshes, and are called Picts from their painting and scoring of wounds that are visible on their bodies. Because they appeared to be painted over with wounds, they were called Picts ('Picti' or 'painted men' in Latin). They and the Goths are of one race; for when the tyrant Maximus left Britain for France to occupy the Empire, the brothers Gratianus and Valentinus (the Emperor's companions) induced these Goths with lavish gifts, flattery, and fair promises to leave Scythia, and to come to the northern region of Britain, because they were stalwart, mighty fighters. In this way these recipients of bribery became settlers and landowners, living in the northern regions where they held cities and towns.

According to Geoffrey of Monmouth, the tyrant Carausius killed Bassianus with the help of the treacherous Picts who had originally come to assist and support Bassianus; and he had granted the Picts a dwelling-place in Albany (Scotland), where they had lived for a long time afterwards and intermarried with the Britons. Ranulph observes that since the Picts first occupied the northern region of Scotland, it appears that the dwelling-place granted to them by Carausius is the southern region of Scotland, stretching from the wall built by the Romans to the Scottish Sea, and containing Galloway, and Lodovia, or Lodway. Bede speaks about this in the following manner: 'The holy man Ninian converted the Southern Picts. Subsequently the Saxons came and annexed the region to Bernicia, the northern division of Northumbria, until the time when Kenneth McAlpine, King of Scotland, expelled the Picts and annexed the land lying between the Tweed and the Scottish Sea to his kingdom.' Bede also relates that a long time afterwards, the Scots were led by Duke Reuda and left Ireland, their own country, and either by alliance or by force established a colony for themselves close to the Picts. This was situated to the north of the inlet of the sea cutting into the land to the west, and formerly separating the Britons and Picts. From this Duke Reuda the Scots took their name, being known as Dalreudines (or

A later antiquarian's impression of the painted and tattooed Picts

The Norman attack on the English army depicted in the Bayeux Tapestry. The Normans are on horseback

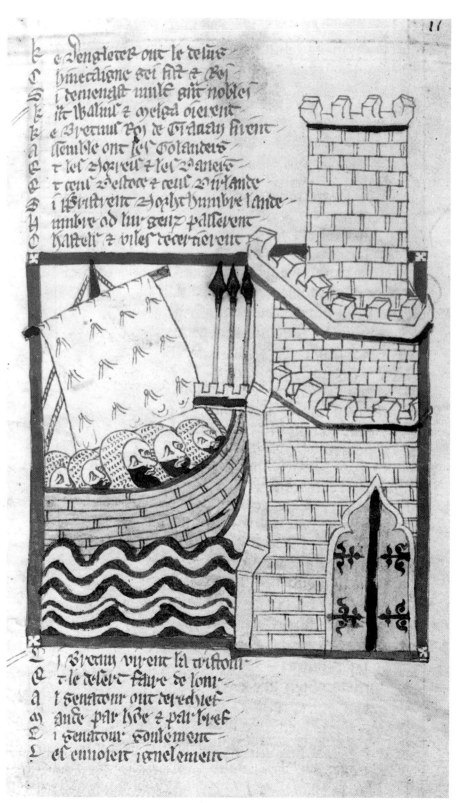

The Scottish invasion of Britain, from an illustration in a mid-fourteenth-century manuscript of The Brut *or 'History of Britain'*

Dalriadans), that is 'Reuda's part', since in their language 'dal' means 'a part'.

Gerald of Wales says that the Picts could obtain no wives amongst the Britons; but took them from amongst the Scots in Ireland, offering them fair promises to live with them and grant them land by the sea, where it is narrow, in the region now called Galloway. Marianus relates that the Scots from Ireland landed in Argyll, that is, Scotsmen's Cliff, intending to inflict harm on the Britons. As Bede says: the Scots, following the Britons and Picts, constituted the third nation inhabiting Briton. Then, as Ranulph relates, the Saxons came at the Britons' request to help them against the Scots and Picts. The Britons were quickly driven out into Wales; and the Saxons occupied the land little by little, and then gradually more and more, as far as the Scottish Sea. In this way the Saxons constituted the fourth kind of people in the island of Britain.

As Bede says, the Saxons and Angles migrated from the continental Germanic homeland, yet some neighbouring Celtic peoples still call them simply 'Germans'. Ranulph adds that nonetheless, in about the year of Our Lord 800, King Egbert of Wessex commanded and proclaimed that everyone should call the inhabitants of this country Englishmen. According to Alfred of Beverley, the Danes subsequently harried the country for about two hundred years; from the time of this Egbert to that of Saint Edward. They constituted the fifth kind of people in the island, though they later declined. Finally, led by Duke William, the Normans came and conquered the English. They still own the land, and form the sixth race in this island.

In the time of King Henry the First, however, many Flemings[2] came and were granted a temporary home near Mailros, to the west of England. They formed the seventh race in the island, though later they were driven out from their home at the same King's command and sent to the neighbourhood of Haverford in West Wales. As Ranulph observes, the Danes and the Picts have quite disappeared now, and five nations remain in Britain: the Scots in Albany or Scotland; the Britons in Cambria or Wales, except for the Flemings in West Wales; and the Normans and English who are intermingled in the whole island. Historical writings leave no doubt about how the Danes were wiped out or expelled from Britain.

The Danish siege of Canterbury, from a glass roundel in the north choir triforium of Canterbury Cathedral

Now for an account of how the Picts were destroyed and declined. According to Gerald of Wales, Britain was formerly occupied by the Saxons and peace was established with the Picts. The Scots, who had come with the Picts, saw that the Picts were nobler in heroic deeds and finer fighters, though they were fewer in number than the Scots. Then the Scots, made envious by that, turned to their native treachery which they have often practised, for they surpass other races in treachery, being naturally disposed to it. They invited all the Picts, and especially their leaders, to a feast, and waited for the moment when the Picts were merry and had drunk a great deal. Suddenly, they pulled away the nails holding up hollow benches beneath the Picts, who all unwary, immediately fell backwards into a marvellously contrived pit. Then the Scots fell upon the Picts and killed them, leaving no one alive. In this way the better warriors from among two races were utterly wiped out, but the others (the Scots), traitors in a manner quite unlike the Picts, profited by that false act of treason; for they took the whole country and still hold it even to the present day, calling it Scotland after themselves. In the time of King Edgar, Kenneth McAlpine was the Duke and leader of the Scots, making war on Pictish territory and destroying the Picts. He attacked the Saxons six times and captured wrongfully all the land between the Tweed and the Scottish Sea.

Chapter Fifteen

THE LANGUAGES, MANNERS AND CUSTOMS OF THE INHABITANTS OF BRITAIN

t has been explained how many races inhabit this island; there is an equal number of languages and dialects. However, the Welsh and Scots, who have not intermingled with the other races, have still kept their language and speech, although those Scots who were once in alliance with the Picts and were living amongst them, have been somewhat influenced by their speech. Yet the Flemings living in West Wales have abandoned their foreign speech and talk like Saxons.

As for the English, although they had three dialects from the beginning: southern, northern and central in the Midlands, since they came from three Germanic tribes; nevertheless by intermingling first with the Danes and then with Normans they have allowed their national language to be corrupted in many respects. Some people stammer oddly, some chatter, others snarl and yet others gnash their teeth with a grating sound. This impairment of the language is caused by two things: one is that schoolchildren first learn to speak English and then are compelled to construe their lessons in French, a practice which has been followed since the Normans came to England; the other is that the children of gentle birth are instructed from their childhood to speak French, and as people from the back of beyond want to ape and imitate gentlemen, they put a lot of effort into speaking French in order to be esteemed more highly. Because of this there is a proverb circulating: 'Jack would be a gentleman if he could speak French.'

John Trevisa comments on these observations by Ranulph that such was the general practice before the Black Death, but that things have recently changed somewhat. John Cornwall, a schoolmaster, altered the practice of grammar-school teaching and substituted construing in English for construing in French. Now other schoolmasters, in the year of Our Lord 1385 or the ninth year of King Richard the Second's reign (John is referring to his own times), follow his practice. They have abandoned all use of French in schools and always practise construing in English. In one respect they gain an advantage, namely that children learn their grammar more quickly, but in another way there is a disadvantage: for now they neither learn nor know any French; which is a hindrance for people who have to travel overseas. Moreover, gentlemen have to a great extent left off teaching their children to speak French.

After John Trevisa's qualification, we return to the comment by Ranulph: that it is a great marvel that the English have such great diversity in the accents and utterance of their own language, confined as it is within one island. The Norman language has come from another country and has only one kind of pronunciation by all those who speak it in England; for people from Kent, the south, the west and the north all speak French with the same accent and pronunciation. John Trevisa adds the qualification that there are as many different kinds of French in the kingdom of France as there are different kinds of English in the kingdom of England. Ranulph goes on to say that there are remarkable aspects of the threefold division of English; for people from the east agree more closely with people from the west in their pronunciation than do people from the north with people from the south.

The firſt of the vij ſciences is gramayre / of whiche for ÿ tyme that is now is not knowen the fourth parte wythout whiche ſcience ſykerly alle other ſciences in eſpecial ben of lytyl recommēdacion by cauſe wythout gramayre ther may none proufyfyte. For gramayre is the fondement and the begynnynge of clergye. & it is the yate by the whiche in thenfancye is be gonne & in contynnyng men come and atteyne to ſapience of clergye. this is the ſcience to fourme the ſpeche be it in la tyn frenſſhe or engliſſh or in ony other langage ÿ mē ſpeke wyth. & who that coude all gramayre he couthe make & conſtrue euery worde. and pnoūce it by exemple god made the worlde by worde/ & the word is to ÿ world ſentence

Here foloweth of lo gyke ca. vij

The ſecond ſciēce is logike whiche is called dyale tyque This

Scenes of school life, from The Treatise to Learn English *printed by Wynkyn de Worde*

For this reason the people of Mercia, who come from Central England, share something with each extreme and understand their neighbouring northern and southern dialects better than northerners and southerners understand each other. William of Malmesbury comments that all the Northumbrian dialects, especially that at York, are so sharp, piercing, grating and ill-formed that southerners (he includes himself) are scarcely able to understand them. He opines that the reason is their proximity to those foreigners who speak strange languages, and also that the Kings of England are based and stay much longer in the south than in the north. They do this because there are better cornlands, more people, more fine cities and more profitable harbours in the south than in the north.

Since the customs and ways of the Welsh and the Scots are described to some extent elsewhere in this book, I now intend to indicate and describe the habits and nature of the intermingled populace of England. The Flemings living in West Wales have now all become just like Englishmen because they live alongside English people: they are mighty, fierce fighters and the greatest enemies the Welsh have; they engage in trading, especially the wool-trade; they are very ready to risk adventure and danger by sea and by land for the sake of great profit; they are willing sometimes to plough the land; and sometimes they engage in deeds of arms as the occasion demands. It appears to be a marvellous attribute of these people that they can tell from a bone of a wether's right shoulder, after the flesh has been boiled off it (not roasted), what has been done, what is being done, and what is to be done; as if by a prophetic spirit or by wondrous art. They discern reliably what is done in distant lands, signs of peace or of war, the state of the realm, and murder and adultery from the signs and tokens on such shoulder-bones.

Ranulph says of the Englishmen inhabiting England that, being intermingled and far from the places from which they first sprang, they turn easily to perverse deeds of their own free will, without being enticed by any other person. And they are so unstable, so impatient of that enemy of activity, peace, and such detesters of sloth that, as William of Malmesbury observes, when they have completely laid low all their enemies, they fight amongst themselves and kill each other; just as an utterly empty stomach

Medieval English culinary activity, showing a duly respectful attitude to food, from the mid-fourteenth-century East Anglian Luttrell Psalter

starts to digest itself. Ranulph observes that, notwithstanding, southerners are more gentle and peaceable than northerners, who are more unstable, cruel, and volatile.

The English share certain characteristics with each of their neighbours and practise gluttony more than others; being inclined to luxury in food and clothing. I think they derive that fault from King Hardicanute,[1] a Dane in origin, who used to order quadruple portions at dinner and supper too. English people are successful both on horseback and on foot, and are ready and able to accomplish all kinds of deeds of arms; they are accustomed to getting the upper hand and winning victory in every fight in which no treason is afoot. They are curious to hear about, and well able to describe, the deeds and marvels they have seen. They travel widely in various countries; there are scarcely any people more wealthy at home or more liberal in distant foreign countries. They are better at obtaining and amassing new wealth than at

A thirteenth-century bronze water jug found in the River Tyne at Hexham depicting a knight on horseback, now in the British Museum

retaining their own inheritances. This is the reason why they are so widely spread and think that every country belongs to them.

The people are apt and astute, but blundering and hasty before the deed and wiser after it than in advance. They give up too easily things they have begun. For this reason, Pope Eugenius[2] said that the English would be capable of doing anything they wished, and of being placed ahead of all the rest, if it were not that their frivolous disposition prevented it. Just as Hannibal said that the Romans could not be overcome except in their homeland, so the English cannot be overcome in foreign countries, though they are easily beaten in their own. Ranulph points out that they despise what is theirs and praise what belongs to others, and are scarcely ever pleased or content with their own condition. Whatever rightly befits and appertains to others they will gladly appropriate to themselves. This is why a yeoman dresses like a squire, a squire like a knight, a knight like a duke and a duke like a king. Others, however, go around wishing to emulate all walks of life, belonging to no rank themselves. For those who are of no social standing are willing to take on any rank: in outward appearance they are minstrels and heralds; great orators in speech; gluttons in eating and drinking; hucksters

A fifteenth-century woodcut depicting the conflict between Sobriety and Gluttony. Whereas in the illustration Sobriety wins, The Description of Britain *declares the English to be gluttonous*

and tavern-keepers in amassing wealth; distinguished men in dress; Argus-like in profitable transactions; Tantalus-like in their labours; Daedalus-like in taking pains; Sardanapalus-like in bed; like graven images in church; sonorous as thunder in court; and owning to being churchmen only when it comes to clerical privileges and income. John Trevisa comments on these Latin names: Argus, Tantalus, Daedalus and Sardanapalus; they are to be understood according to the fictions[3] which poets have written about them. Argus was a herdsman who watched over animals and had a hundred eyes (the name can also refer to a ship, a mariner or a merchant); he was therefore able to see in front of, behind and all around himself. Therefore the man who is prudent, wary, and alert to deception may fittingly be called an Argus, and so the *Polychronicon* uses the plural, saying that Englishmen are Arguses, to signify that they are sharp-eyed where profit is to be had. The second name, Tantalus, comes from a poetical fiction in which Tantalus killed his own son and was thereby damned to everlasting punishment: he stands eternally in water up to his lower lip, and ripe apples and splendid fruit hang down all the time just to his upper lip, but neither fruit nor water can enter his mouth because of the way in which he is confined; he is placed between food and drink and yet he can neither eat nor drink; and he is always so hungry and thirsty that his state is piteous. Because of their resemblance to Tantalus, people who do absolutely nothing where a great deal is there to be done in all directions are called Tantaluses, apparently to indicate that they are Tantalus-like in work because they get nothing done. The third name, Daedalus, should make us note that Daedalus was a subtle, devious man, so that such people are called after him on account of their resemblance to him. The fourth name, Sardanapalus, reminds us that Sardanapalus was the King of the Assyrians and a most unchaste man, accustomed to lie in luxurious beds. So, because of their resemblance to him, unchaste lovers are labelled with his name.

Ranulph observes that amongst the entire intermingled English nation there is such variation and diversity of clothes and fashion, and there are so many different looks and lines that scarcely anyone can be placed in his true rank from his clothing and dress. For this reason a holy anchorite prophesied

Devotion to dress: a man being dressed by his servants, from the early fourteenth-century Queen Mary's Psalter

in King Egilfred's[4] time in the following terms:

Because the English are so inclined to drunkenness, treason, and disrespect for the house of God, they shall be conquered: first by the Danes; then by the Normans; and in the third instance by the Scots, whom they consider to be the greatest wretches and the lowest of the low. Then the world will be so unstable and changeable that inward instability will be manifest outwardly in the multiplicity and diversity of men's clothing.

Chapter Sixteen

WALES

ow this book will deal with Wales after England, so I transfer my attention and travel into Wales, to the noble race descended from Priam's[1] blood, in order to acquire knowledge of great Jupiter's descendants and to commemorate the Trojan race. I shall take four headings: I shall attempt to describe the condition of the land (praising it warmly) and the origins of the populace, then I shall describe with my pen all the customs of the people, and then I shall try to describe all the country's marvels.

Chapter Seventeen

WHY IT IS CALLED WALES

ales is now called Wallia. It was formerly called Cambria because Camber, Brutus's son, was its Prince and lived there. Then it became Wallia after Queen Gwalaes, child of King Ebrancus.[1] If you take the name of the lord Gwalon and remove the first consonant and the ending, adding '-lia', you will get 'Wallia'. Although the country is much smaller than England, it contains equally good land; just as a daughter takes after her mother.

The fine remains of the Archbishop's Palace at St David's

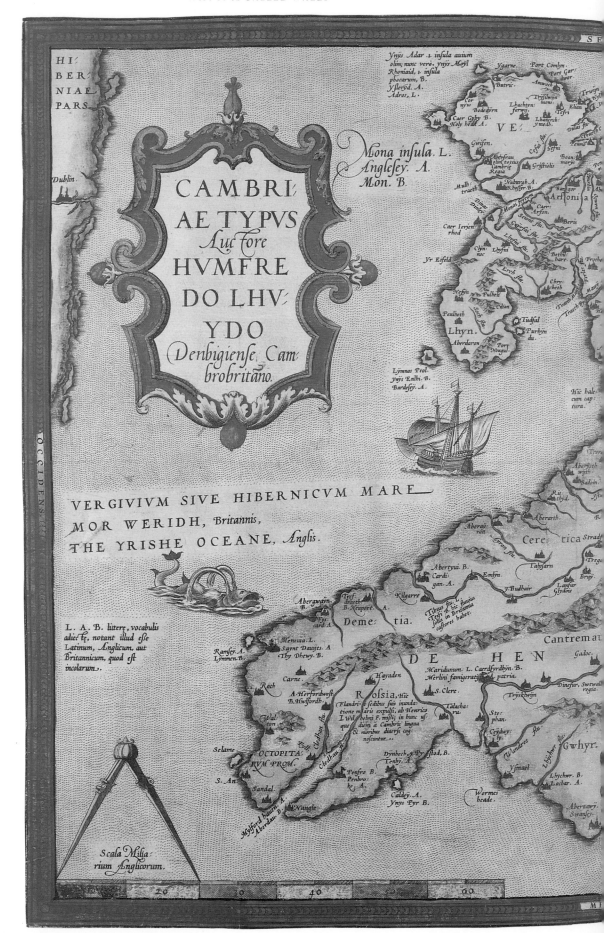

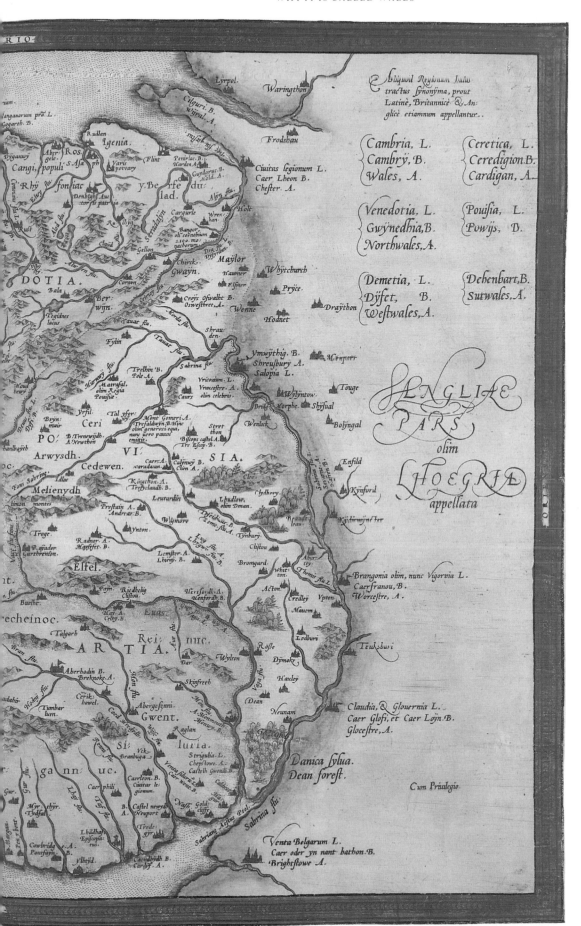

{ Aliquid Regionum huius
tractus synonyma, prout
Latinè, Britannicè & An:
glicè etiamnum appellantur.

{ Cambria, L.
{ Cambrÿ, B.
{ Wales, A.

{ Ceretica, L.
{ Ceredigion. B.
{ Cardigan, A.

{ Venedotia, L.
{ Gwÿnedhia, B.
{ Northwales, A.

{ Pouisia, L.
{ Powÿs, D.

{ Demetia, L.
{ Dÿfet, B.
{ Westwales, A.

{ Dehenbart, B.
{ Sutwales, A.

ANGLIÆ
PARS
olim
LHOEGRIA
appellata

Cum Priuilegio.

Chapter Eighteen

THE ATTRIBUTES OF WALES

 lthough the country is small, it is full of corn and fruit. There is also a great abundance of meat, fish, tame and wild beasts, horses, sheep, and gentle oxen, and it is an excellent land for growing all kinds of seeds, corn, grass, and creeping plants. There are rivers and springs, hills which provide excellent metals, and valleys which give rise to waterways. There are coal-formations under the ground with grass growing on top on all sides, and lime is abundant there, as are roofing-materials. There is plenty of fine white milk and various choice honeys. The valleys are well-provided with sweet mead and ale. The land brings forth in richness whatever is necessary to sustain life. But let me describe all these great riches in as few words as possible: it is a remote corner, as though in the beginning God had first created the land so fertile as to dispense all possible beneficial things. Wales is divided by a river called Twy, which separates North and South Wales in well-known places. The south is called Demetia and the north Venedocia. In the north, shooting with bows and arrows is practised, whereas in the south, only spears are used. There were formerly three courts in Wales: one at Carmarthen; the second in Anglesey; and the third in Powys at Pengwern, now Shrewsbury. There used to be seven bishops in Wales, but these days there are only four, and they are now subject to Saxon authority, though formerly their bishoprics were subordinate to the Princes of Wales.

Previous page: A late medieval map of Wales, from the British Library

The memorial brass of Robert Greyndour (1443) depicting a miner from the Forest of Dean, bordering on Wales, carrying his pick, candle and hod

Nan Gwywant Pass, with Moel Hebog looming in the distance and fertile valley-land in the middle ground

The 'Snowy Mountains': a winter scene showing Tryfan Mountain in Snowdonia

Chapter Nineteen

THE CUSTOMS AND RITUALS OF THE WELSH

he way of life in Wales is very different from that in England in matters of food, drink, dress, and in many other aspects. The people are extremely well-dressed in a shirt, mantle, and an excellent pair of trousers to protect them against the wind and rain. In this garb they brave the weather, even though it is extremely cold. They always go about in this garb; fighting, amusing themselves, leaping, standing, sitting, and even sleeping without sheets all the time. The people walk about without surcotes, gowns, coats, overmantles, gipouns, tabards, cloaks, wraps, belts, or headgear such as hoods, hats or caps to cover themselves with, and they are always bare-legged. They practise no other way of going about even if they are to meet the King. They fight with arrows and short spears against anyone who harms them, and when the need arises they fight better on foot than on horseback. Instead of castles and towers, they take woodlands and marshes as defensible strongholds. When they think the moment is ripe they will flee from a battle. Gildas says the Welsh are unstable and not to be relied on for peace. When people ask the reason, it is hardly any wonder that people expelled from their own land should attempt to expel others. However, it has

Welsh diversions: a hunting-scene of greyhounds pursuing a stag, depicted on medieval floor-tiles from Neath Abbey

A Welsh bowman in shirt and mantle, barelegged and, inexplicably, shod on one foot only

all been for nothing, since now many woodlands have been felled and mighty castles have been built beside the sea.

The people are capable of going for a long time without food and greatly like their native foodstuffs; they know how to eat and enjoy themselves without elaborate cookery. They eat hot and cold barley-bread and oatcakes; these being wide, round, thin biscuits, which they find very suitable for so

The figure of Christ, from the cover of The Book of Llandaff, *showing the Welsh capacity for sensibility to the fine arts as well as for the material things of life*

great a race. They rarely eat wheat-bread or cook in ovens. They have a kind of gruel for soup, accompanied by leeks, butter, milk, and cheese shaped oblong and in blocks. They eat such concoctions eagerly; this causes them to drink mead and strong ale in large quantities; often all day and all night. The redder the wine, the more highly they esteem it. They tell many idle stories; for when they are occupied with drinking they are full of talk. Both at and after meals they greatly enjoy salt and leeks. Householders customarily regard it as very fitting to dispense bowls of soup to people whom they invite for meals; they share out the food at mealtimes, giving everyone his portion and retaining any surplus for their own consumption. When they have the

David, the Old Testament king and psalmist, depicted in an early sixteenth-century Jesse tree window in St Dyfnog's Church, Llanrhaeadr. His traditional association with the harp endeared him to the Welsh

The Welsh vegetable par excellence: *harvesting leeks, from a fifteenth-century manuscript*

THE CUSTOMS AND RITUALS OF THE WELSH

misfortune to be short of meat, they always eat hot salmon, however much the doctor may forbid it.

Their houses are low, constructed of small wooden rods, and are not placed close together as in cities, but are far apart and not over-high. When everything at home has been eaten up, they will move on to their neighbours to eat whatever they can see and find, and then return home. They lead an idle life, burning things for warmth, sleeping and doing other such things. Welshmen have a regular custom of washing their guests' feet at night; if their feet are washed all over, they know themselves to be welcome. They live together in such comfort that they hardly ever carry a purse around. Whether at home or out, they keep their money and their comb suspended from their breeches. It is remarkable that they are so fastidious, detesting farting, when they do not balk at depositing their own excrement at their very doors.

At great banquets they have harps, tabors, and pipes to provide music. They carry corpses in procession with great lamentation, blowing loudly on goats' horns. They greatly esteem Trojan blood, since they are all descended from it. They are fond of observing family relationships, even when distant to the hundredth degree. They set themselves up above others, though they greatly venerate priests, and honour Almighty God's servants like heavenly angels.

This race has often been deceived into desiring battle madly, by the prophecies of Merlin and by enchantment. The beastly manners of these Celts have now been improved by contact with the Saxons, as is manifestly recognized. They cultivate gardens, fields, and slopes, and congregate together in pleasant towns. They ride about fully armed, wearing breeches and shoes. They sit pleasantly at their meals and sleep in many a comfortable bed. To anyone considering them, they seem more like Englishmen than Welshmen nowadays. If people should wish to know the reason, it is because they now live at peace more than they were formerly accustomed to do, because of their prosperity, for their possessions would be diminished if they often got involved in conflicts. The fear of losing what they have has now made them peaceable. It has been well put in an aphorism: 'Own nothing,

133

fear nothing.' The Roman satirist, Juvenal,[1] gives a terse illustration: 'The penniless traveller sings in the presence of the robber, being bolder on his journey than the fine rich fellow on horseback.'

Chapter Twenty

THE MARVELS AND WONDERS OF WALES

here is a pool at Brecknock containing many shoals of fish; it often changes colour on the surface, being covered by vegetation. It often happens that the shapes of buildings can be discerned in it. When the pool is frozen over, marvellous noises can be heard beneath it. If the Prince of Wales comes, the birds sing very pleasant melodies as delightfully as they can, but they will sing for no one else.

Near Caerleon, two miles outside the city, there stands a rock which shines brilliantly with the sun on it; it is known as Golden Cliff, because it shines as bright as gold. Such a flower amongst rocks can scarcely be without fruit if men were to seek for gold, for if the veins of the earth were to be opened by human skill, many natural resources now hidden from human scrutiny would be revealed; though they yet remain unknown because of men's lack of ingenuity. Great treasure is concealed in the earth and will be found in days to come as a result of the great effort and labour of those who are to follow us. What men of old acquired by necessity comes to us by our diligent efforts. As John Trevisa observes, one can read in books how nature never fails at need: when men's minds were devoid of skill, God and nature helped to provide it; when no teacher existed, men acquired skill from God. Those who acquired skill in this way taught it to other people. Certain skills as yet undiscovered will be acquired by some men with God's grace.

Ranulph tells us of an island filled with noise and disturbance in West Wales at Cardiff, near to the bank of the Severn; it is called Barry. On the side closest to the mainland a marvellous noise and uproar can be heard if you put

One of the numerous small islands off the rugged Welsh coast, Bardsey Island, Gwynedd – home of monks and traditionally the burial place of Merlin

Another problem for King Vortigern: being trapped in a burning castle, from an illustration to Peter Langtoft's fourteenth-century Chronicle of England

your ear to a fissure. The sounds of leaves and wind, metallic sounds such as the rubbing of iron on whetstones and the sound of ovens being heated up by flames are to be heard. All this may well be caused by waves breaking beneath it with such noises and disturbances. In certain places at Pembroke, demons often bring about evil, introducing foul things and scorning the notion of sin. Neither skill nor prayers can remove that affliction; when it is plaguing the country it bodes sorrow for the inhabitants. At Crug Mawr in West Wales there is a marvellous burial-place; it seems to be the same size as everyone who comes to see it. An undamaged weapon left on it overnight will be broken before daylight. At Nefyn in North Wales there is a small island called Bardsey where monks still live. People live so long in that region that the oldest always die first. Merlin, also called Silvestris, is reputedly buried there.

There are two Merlins who both uttered prophecies; one was called Merlin Ambrosius and was begotten by a goblin at Carmarthen in Demetia in the reign of King Vortigern. He uttered his prophecies in Snowdonia at the source of the River Conway, on the side of Mount Eryri, or Dinas Emrys in Welsh, and Ambrosius's Mount in English. King Vortigern sat at the water's edge, full of anxiety. There and then Merlin Ambrosius prophesied in his presence. John Trevisa speculates on how anyone could believe that a fiend could now beget a child. In the opinion of some people, he is incapable of it. The demon who often goes about at night to betray women is properly called

Merlin Ambrosius uttering prophecies to King Uther Pendragon, father of King Arthur, again from Peter Langtoft's Chronicle of England

A view of the stream to Llyn Dinas, Dinas Emrys, in Gwynedd. 'Emrys' is the Welsh form of 'Ambrosius'. The site is also known as 'Vortigern's Mount'

an incubus; the kind which betrays men is called a succubus. God defend us from any such evil things! Whoever falls into their clutches is in no happy condition. By a supernatural process fiends skilfully preserve and bring together the seed of men and women, and in this way they can cause women to bear children. Yet never since time immemorial has there been a child descended from a demon, for, incontrovertibly, no such child would be able to die. Scholarship reminds us that death cannot kill any fiend, but death destroyed Merlin, so obviously he was not of demonic origin.

There was a second Merlin from Albany (now Scotland), and he was known by two additional names: Silvestris, and Calidonius after the Caledonian forest where he uttered his prophecies. He was also called Silvestris because when he was in a battle, he saw something terrifying in the sky and immediately went mad, remaining not an instant longer but fleeing to the wood. John Trevisa explains that Silvestris means 'belonging to a wood' or else 'distracted' or else 'living in a wood'. Ranulph relates that Merlin Silvestris uttered good and very accurate prophecies in King Arthur's reign; more plainly and less obscurely than Merlin Ambrosius.

There are marvellously high mountains in Snowdonia, as tall as a man can climb in a day; they are called Eryri in Welsh and the Snowy Mountains in English. In these mountains there is enough pasture for all the animals in Wales. At the top there are two huge fish-pools. One of the lakes contains an island which is moved by the wind as if it were floating and comes close to the bank, so that herdsmen are greatly amazed and think that the earth is moving beneath them. In the other lake there are perch and other fish, all with only one eye, a phenomenon also found in the Mulwell in Scotland. On the boundary of Rhuddlan there is a small spring which does not ebb and flow like the sea, twice daily, but which is sometimes empty and sometimes brimful. In North Wales, in Mon or Anglesey, there is a rock resembling a man's thigh; no matter how far anyone carries it away, it returns to its starting-place at night. Hugh, the Earl of Shrewsbury, proved that by personal experience during the reign of Henry the First; because he wanted to discover the truth of the matter, he bound the stone to another with strong iron chains, and threw them, fettered together, into deep water. Yet,

St Winifred's Well, then in the care of the Abbey at Basingwerk, at Holywell in Clwyd, where the virgin saint is reputed to have had her throat cut

early next morning, the stone was seen in Anglesey. A peasant, considering himself to be very crafty, bound this stone to his thigh, but before daybreak his thigh had gone septic and the stone had vanished. If acts of lechery are committed near the stone it exudes moisture, and no child will be conceived. There is also a marvellous rock called 'the rock of hearing', named on the *lucus a non lucendo* principle: if anyone shouts or blows a horn or makes any other noise, it renders everything inaudible.

There is another island close to Anglesey where there are numerous hermits. If any of them should quarrel, innumerable mice come and devour all their food; this misfortune does not cease until the dispute is over. Just as the inhabitants of this land are as irascible as those of Ireland, so its saints are quick to exact vengeance. Just as in Ireland and Scotland, in Wales bells and crooked staves are held in veneration by clerics and laymen, who feel as much awe about swearing on either of them as on the Bible. There is a well at Basingwerk popularly called 'Sacer' or 'holy', which surges so vigorously that it flings back anything thrown into it, as anyone may witness. So much water flows from it that it would adequately supply the whole country. Sick people receive both healing and divine grace there. Speckled red stones are frequently found in its waters, betokening the red blood shed by the virgin Winifred when her throat was cut at the well. The man who did the deed has a curse on his descendants; his children will perpetually bark like puppies and dogs until they pray for that maiden's grace; either at the spring itself or in Shrewsbury where she rests in peace.

Chapter Twenty-One

SCOTLAND

t is commonly said that the country now called Scotland is a projection of the northern part of Great Britain and is separated from Britain by inlets of the sea at its southern end (being surrounded by the sea everywhere else). It was formerly called Albany after its first settler Albanactus, son of King Brutus, or else after the province Albania, a region of Scythia, close to the country of the Amazons; hence the name of the Scots, or as one might say, the 'Sciti', who come from Scythia. Afterwards the country was known as Pictavia because the Picts held sway there for a thousand and seventy years or, according to some accounts, one thousand three hundred and sixty years. Finally it was known as Hibernia, just like Ireland. Gerald of Wales gives several reasons for this. The first is the affinity and closeness existing between the inhabitants of Scotland and the Irish, since they took wives from Ireland; something that can be seen patently in their religion, clothing, language and speech, weapons and customs. A second reason is that Irishmen formerly settled in Scotland.

Bede relates that Irishmen came from Ireland, the homeland of the Scots, with their leader Reuda and, either by alliance or by force, established major settlements and cities near the Picts in the north. Gerald observes that the country is now simply called Scotland after the Scots who came from Ireland and held sway there for three hundred and fifteen years until the time of William the Red, brother of Malcolm. Ranulph points to the large amount of evidence available that Scotland is often called and referred to as Hibernia just like Ireland. Bede says that Laurence, Archbishop of Canterbury, was the Archbishop of the Scots and lived in an island called Hibernia adjacent to Britain. Bede also says that an epidemic amongst the livestock brought Hibernia low and that the Scots inhabited the southern region of Hibernia. He tells us that Chad,[1] as a youth, was instructed in the monastic rule in Hibernia, and that Egfrith, King of Northumbria, laid waste Hibernia. Yet again, Bede refers to 'the majority of the Scots in Hibernia', and in the same chapter he distinguishes between Hibernia proper, the island a hundred miles west of Britain and separated from it by the sea, and the Hibernia which is now Scotland. There he relates how Adamnan,[2] the Abbot of Iona, sailed to Hibernia to instruct the Irish about the lawful date of Easter, and finally returned to Scotland. Isidore of Seville says in his *Etymologies* that the inhabitants of Scotland are called Scots in their own language, and also Picts, because their bodies used to be 'painted' in the following manner: they used to incise and prick their own bodies with a sharp-edged tool, marking out

An eighth-century cross-slab, standing in the churchyard at Aberlemno, illustrating Pictish warriors

The Kildalton Cross at Kildalton, Islay, showing the affinities between the Celtic art of Scotland and of Ireland

various figures and shapes on them which they stained with ink or other pigments and colours, so that they were called 'Picti', which means 'painted men' in Latin.

The Scots are frivolous, and very alien and wild, though by intermingling with the English they have been much improved. They are cruel to their enemies and loathe captivity above all things; they consider it disgraceful sloth if a man dies in his bed and a great distinction if he dies on the battlefield. They eat frugally and are capable of fasting for a long time, eating very little whilst the sun is up. They eat meat, fish, fruit, and milk more than bread. Although they are very beautifully formed they are made repellent and extremely ugly by their own clothing. They are very enthusiastic about the customs of their own ancestors and scornful about other people's achievements. Their country is very fertile, with pastureland, gardens, and fields.

The Scottish princes, like the Spanish kings, are not customarily anointed or crowned. In Scotland, Saint Andrew the Apostle is held in great and solemn veneration. The northern regions of the world and the Scythians and Picts were allotted to him as his portion; so that he might preach to the people and convert them to faith in Christ. He was finally martyred in Achaia in Greece, in a city called Patras, where his bones were kept for two hundred and seventy-two years until the time of the Emperor Constantine.[3] Subsequently, they were translated to Constantinople and kept there for a hundred and ten years until the time of the Emperor Theodosius.[4] Then Ungus, King of the Picts in Scotland, laid waste a large area of Britain and was surrounded by a great army of Britons in a field called Merk, and he heard Saint Andrew speak to him like this: 'Ungus, Ungus, listen to me, the apostle of Christ. I promise you help and succour. When you have overcome your enemies by my help, you must render a third of your inheritance as alms to

A carved footprint in the Dark Age fortress of Dunadd, near Kilmartin, Argyll

The ruins of the Cathedral at St Andrews, Fife, where the church in honour of the martyred apostle was founded

Almighty God and in honour of Saint Andrew.' The sign of the cross was carried before his army, and on the third day he won the victory and so returned home, dividing his inheritance as he had been bidden. Since he was uncertain what city to assign to Saint Andrew he fasted for three days, and he and his men prayed the saint to show them what place was his choice. One of the guardians who watched over the body of Saint Andrew in Constantinople was warned in a dream to go to a place to which an angel would lead him, and so he reached Scotland with seven companions, going to the top of a hill called Ragmund. At that very moment a light shone from heaven and surrounded the King of the Picts on his way to a place called Carcenan. Soon after that, many sick men were healed. In that place the King met Regulus, the monk from Constantinople who was carrying Saint Andrew's relics. A church, the chief amongst all the churches in the land of the Picts, or Scotland, was founded there in honour of Saint Andrew. Pilgrims come to this church from all nations. Regulus was the first abbot of this foundation and gathered monks together in it. For this reason he was the one who shared out the tithe of land which the King had assigned to him amongst abbeys all over the country.

Chapter Twenty-Two

IRELAND

ibernia is another name for Ireland, which, since ancient times has been subsumed under the dominion of Britain, according to Gerald of Wales in his *History and Topography of Ireland*, where he gives a full account of it. It is nonetheless fitting to praise the land more extensively. The following chapters clear the way towards clear and full acquaintance with the country. I shall therefore describe its location and position, its size and nature, its endowments and deficiencies, and its earliest inhabitants. I shall also speak of the customs of its inhabitants, of its marvels and the excellence of the saints and holy men of that nation.

Chapter Twenty-Three

THE BOUNDARIES OF IRELAND

reland is the last of all the islands in the west. It took its name Hibernia from a certain Hiberus,[1] Hermon's brother, because these two brothers obtained the country by conquest. Alternatively, it is called Hibernia after the River Hiberus in the western region of Spain. Ireland is also known as Scotland because the Scots inhabited it formerly before they reached the other Scotland which is now part of Britain. It is for this reason that we find recorded in the *Martyrology*: 'on a certain day Saint Bridget was born in Scotland' (meaning Ireland). To the south-east lies Spain, a three days' journey by ship, to the west the limitless Ocean, the sea surrounding the earth, and to the north lies Iceland, also three days' journey by ship. The sea between Ireland and Britain is, however, full of huge waves and turbulent all year, so that people can rarely sail across in safety. The sea is a hundred and twenty miles wide.

Chapter Twenty-Four

IRELAND'S GREATNESS AND QUALITIES

reland is the largest island after Britain and stretches northwards from the hills of Saint Brendan to the island called Columbina; to walk its length takes eight days in forty-mile stints. From Dublin to the hills of Saint Patrick and the neighbouring sea it is four days' journey in forty-mile stints. Ireland is narrower in the middle than at the ends, quite the opposite of Britain; just as Ireland is shorter to the north than Britain, so is it proportionately longer to the south. The country is not flat, but full of mountains, hills, woods, marshes and moorland; it is mild, rainy and windy. By the sea it is low-lying and in the interior, hilly and sandy. According to Solinus there is a great abundance of

fine pasture and grazing. As a result of this, the animals must frequently be driven out of their pasture for fear they should eat too much, as they would do themselves harm if they were allowed to eat as much as they wished. Gerald of Wales notes that whilst the native inhabitants commonly retain their health, strangers often suffer from a dangerous flux there because of the moisture in the food. In Ireland beef is wholesome and pork unwholesome. The inhabitants do not suffer from fever, but only from a feverish ague, and then only rarely; therefore the wholesomeness and salubriousness of that country is worth all the splendour and riches of woods, herbs, spices, luxurious fabrics, and precious stones from the Orient. The cause of the wholesomeness and salubriousness of Ireland is its temperate climate.

Ireland is well endowed with the following commodities: in it there are more cattle than oxen; more pastureland than cornfields; and more grass than wheat. There is great abundance of salmon, lampreys, eels and other sea-fish; of eagles, cranes, peacocks, curlews, sparrowhawks, goshawks, and noble falcons; of wolves, and of very troublesome mice. There are spiders,

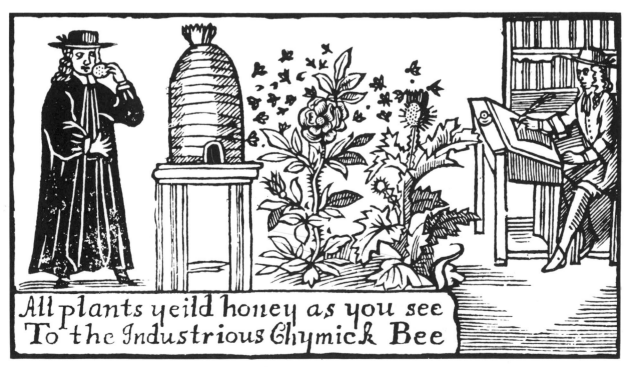

A beehive, shown in a woodcut. The technology of beekeeping has remained fairly constant throughout the centuries

Barnacle geese were believed to grow on trees. Because of this monks were allowed to eat them on fasting days. From Gerald of Wales's Topographica Hibernica

leeches and ants (which cause no harm), and weasels, which are slender in body but very valiant and strong. There are barnacle geese like wild geese, which grow miraculously on trees, as if Nature were breaking her own laws. Monks eat barnacle geese on fasting-days, because they were not begotten by fleshly procreation, in which respect it seems to me they are in error, for it is contrary to reason. For if a man ate Adam's leg, he would have eaten flesh, and yet Adam was not begotten of a father and mother; that flesh took its origin miraculously from the earth, and similarly this flesh is miraculously derived from the tree.

In Ireland there is great abundance of honey, milk, wine, and vineyards. Solinus and Isidore record that Ireland has no bees; notwithstanding, it would be more accurate to record that Ireland has bees, but no vineyards! Also, Bede records that a great deal of roebuck-hunting takes place, even though it is well known that there is none. It is scarcely to be wondered at in Bede since he never set eyes on the country; someone spun him a yarn. There are also beautiful stones in Ireland: the saxagonus or iris (if that stone is held against the sun it immediately forms a rainbow); a stone called gagates (or jet); and white pearls.

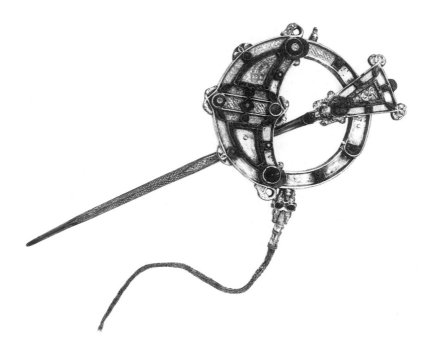

The Tara brooch with its 'beautiful stones', now in the National Museum of Ireland. It was found in a wooden box with several Viking objects at Bettystown, Co. Meath

Chapter Twenty-Five

IRELAND'S DEFICIENCIES

n Ireland, the grains of wheat are very small and difficult to clean by hand. With the exception of human beings, all animals are smaller than in other countries. Almost all kinds of freshwater fish are lacking, as are crossbred falcons, gerfalcons, partridges, pheasants, nightingales and magpies; nor are there any roes, bucks, hedgehogs, polecats, or poisonous creatures. For this reason some people pretend and say to Saint Patrick's credit that he cleansed the land of snakes and venomous beasts, but it is more probable and reasonable that Ireland has always been without such snakes from the beginning, for venomous beasts and snakes die there immediately if they are brought from other countries. Similarly, venom and poison brought there from other countries lose their harmfulness as soon as they are halfway across the sea. Moreover, dust and earth from Ireland, when strewn and spread in other countries, drive off snakes to such an extent that if a turf from Ireland is wrapped around a snake, it kills it or causes it to bore through the earth to escape. Cocks crow only a short time before daylight in Ireland, so that the

An early sixteenth-century woodcut showing events from the life of St Patrick, including, on the right, his opening of an entrance to Purgatory

first cock-crow there and the third cock-crow in other countries happen at the same hour before the dawn.

Chapter Twenty-Six

THE FIRST INHABITANTS OF IRELAND

erald of Wales says that Casera, Noah's grandchild, was afraid of the Flood, and fled with three men and fifty women to Ireland, becoming the first inhabitants in the last year before Noah's Flood. Afterwards, however, Bartholanus, son of Sere, who was descended from Japhet (Noah's son), went there with his three sons by chance or design three hundred years after Noah's Flood, and dwelt there, increasing to nine thousand in number. Later, because of the rotting stench of the corpses of some giants they had killed, they all died except for one, Ruanus. He survived one thousand five hundred years until Saint Patrick's time and informed the holy man about the people we have just mentioned and about all their deeds. Then in the third place Nymeth came to Ireland from Scythia with his four sons and lived there for two hundred and sixteen years, but in the end, because of various misfortunes such as wars and epidemics, they became completely extinct, and the land remained empty for two hundred years afterwards.

The fourth settlement took place when five dukes, Gandius, Genandius, Segandius, Rutheragus and Slanius, all brothers and descendants of Nymeth, came from Greece and occupied Ireland, dividing it into five parts each containing twelve candreds. They placed a stone in the middle of the country, as if in its navel, signifying the beginning of the five kingdoms. Finally, Slanius was made king of the whole country. The fifth settlement happened when the nation had been united for thirty years and had grown weak; four noble men, sons of King Millesius,[1] came from Spain with many companions in a fleet of sixty ships. Two of the noblest of these four brothers, Hiberus and Hermon, divided the country between them; but afterwards, the agreement between them was broken and Hiberus was killed. Then Hermon was king of the whole country. From his time until that of the first Patrick there were a hundred and thirty-one kings of Ireland. So, from the coming of the Hibernienses until the first Patrick, one thousand eight hundred years elapsed. They took the names 'Hibernienses' and 'Hibernia' from Hiberus, mentioned earlier, or else from the river in Spain called Hiberus. They were also called Gaitels and Scots after a certain Gaitelus,[2] nephew of Phenius, who could speak many languages after the diversification of languages at the tower of Nemproth (or Babel). He married Scotta, Pharaoh's daughter.

From these rulers the Hibernienses are descended. People say that Gaitelus invented the Irish language and called it 'Gaitelaf', signifying a language assembled from all languages and tongues. Finally, Belinus, King of Britain, had a son called Gurguntius, who on leaving Denmark found men called Basclenses in the Orkneys, who had come there from Spain and who prayed and entreated to be granted somewhere to live. The King sent them to Ireland, which was then empty and deserted, and commissioned and sent

Noah and his family, reputedly the first inhabitants of Ireland. A carving from Lincoln Cathedral

A Viking figurine, most likely a chess-piece, carved from an antler-tip and found in Dublin. Caxton believed Dublin to have been founded by the Norwegians

with them dukes and captains of his own. Hence it appears that Ireland should belong to Britain by ancient right. From the time of the first Saint Patrick until that of King Fedlimidius,[3] thirty-three kings reigned in succession in Ireland.

In Fedlimidius's time, Duke Turgesius, leader of the Norwegians, took men from Norway to Ireland, occupying it and constructing in many places deep earthworks and single, double, and even treble fortifications, as well as mightily walled strongholds, a lot of which still stand entire. The Irish, however, have no use for castles, for they use woodlands as their castles and take marshes and bogs for the ditches around castles. In the end Turgesius died by means of women's deceitful tricks, and the English say that Gurmundus[4] conquered Ireland and constructed those very ditches, making no mention of Turgesius, but the Irish tell of Turgesius and know nothing about Gurmundus. Therefore it is to be inferred that Gurmundus had conquered and settled in Britain, and that he despatched Turgesius with a mighty force to Ireland to conquer it; and because Turgesius was the captain and leader of that expedition, and seen by the Irish, they tell a great deal about him as a nobleman well known in their country. When Gurmundus had finally been killed in France, Turgesius fell in love with the daughter of the King of Meath in Ireland, and her father promised him that he would send her to him with fifteen maidens at the lake called Lough Owel, where Turgesius promised to meet her with fifteen of the noblest men he had. He kept his promise, suspecting no guile, but fifteen beardless young men came there, dressed as women but with short swords concealed beneath their clothes. They fell on Turgesius, killing him on the spot; and in this way he was destroyed by treachery after ruling for thirty years.

Not long afterwards, three brothers, Amelanus, Siracus, and Ivorus, travelled to Ireland from Norway with their men, ostensibly for the sake of peaceful trade, and settled on the sea-coast with the consent of the Irish, who have always been as idle as the Knights of Saint Paul. The Norwegians built three cities there: Dublin, Waterford, and Limerick. Their numbers increased rapidly, and they rebelled against the native population. They were the first to bring battle-axes to Ireland. So, from the time of Turgesius until that of King Roderick of Connaught, the last King of the whole of Ireland, there were seventeen kings, and the total number of kings to reign there between the time of the first, Hermon, and the last, Roderick, was one hundred and eighty-one. Kings were not as yet crowned or anointed, nor did they succeed each other by the law of inheritance, but by might and superiority and power in war. King Henry the Second of England, in the fortieth year of his life and the seventeenth of his reign, subjugated Roderick in the year of Our Lord 1172.

Chapter Twenty-Seven

THE NATURE AND WAYS OF THE IRISH

olinus says that the people of this country are barbarians; prone to aggression and great fighters, but unable to discern right from wrong. They wear primitive clothing and are poorly supplied with provisions, they are cruel-hearted and sharp-spoken, and they first drink the blood of men who have met a violent death and then wash their faces with it. They are satisfied with meat and fruit for food and with milk for drink. They habitually indulge in many diversions, such as idleness and hunting, but they do very little work. In their childhood they are nourished and fed in hardship, and they are uncultivated in their manners and dress; wearing woollen breeches and leggings, narrow hoods which hang down a cubit over their shoulders behind their backs, and wraps instead of mantles and cloaks. Moreover, they do not use saddles, boots, or spurs when they ride, but urge on their horses with a rod trimmed at the upper end. Instead of cutting and restrictive bits and bridles, they use a form of bridle which does not prevent horses from eating their feed. They fight unarmed and naked; nonetheless they use pairs of short javelins, spears, and broad battle-axes, and fight using one hand.

The Irish refuse to till the soil, but watch over pastureland for their beasts. They cultivate long beards, and long tresses hang down their backs. They practise no crafts of weaving linen or wool, or of metalwork or trading, but give themselves up to idleness and sloth, as they consider rest their pleasure and freedom their wealth.

Although Scotland, Ireland's daughter, may use the harp, psaltery and tabor, the Irishmen themselves are skilled at two kinds of musical instrument: the harp and the psaltery strung with brass strings. With these instruments, although they play speedily and rapidly, they produce very pleasant harmonies and melodies with very heavily ornamented tunes, phrases, and airs. They start from B flat[1] and play very quietly with a muted sound in the lower strings, returning to the note from which they started.

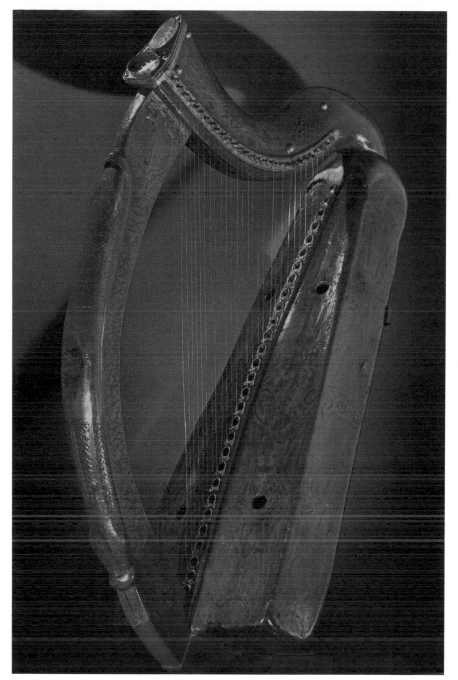

The so-called 'Harp of Brian Boru' — one of the instruments the Irish excelled at playing, according to Caxton

Thus the greatest part of their artistry hides that artistry, apparently as if the skill so concealed would be ashamed to be revealed.

The Irish maintain bad customs in their way of life: they pay no tithes; they do not marry lawfully; they do not even refrain from incest, but one brother will marry another's wife; they readily betray their neighbours and others; they carry battle-axes in their hands instead of staffs, and use them for fighting against the people who trust them most. They are fickle, volatile, and sly traitors. Anyone having anything to do with them needs to fear guile more than skill, peace more than incendiary firebrands, honey more than gall, and malice more than chivalry from them. Their ways are such that they are not strong in warfare and fighting, or true in peace; they become godparents to those whom they quite treacherously betray in that sanctified relationship between godparents and godchildren.[2] Each man drinks other men's blood when it is shed. To some extent they love their nurslings and playfellows who were suckled by the same milk which nourished them as children, but they persecute their brothers, cousins, and other kinsmen. They scorn their living kinsmen and yet avenge their deaths when they are killed. So long has the practice of evil ways endured amongst them that it has overmastered them and transformed treacherousness into a natural attribute, making them born traitors. Foreigners and people from abroad living amongst them follow their customs, so that there is scarcely anyone who is not besmirched with their treacherousness.

A contentious and treacherous-looking Irishman killing another with a battle-axe, from a manuscript of Gerald of Wales's Topographica Hibernica

Antiquarians' impressions of Irish garb; the figure on the right was reproduced in a nineteenth-century engraving from Speed's Map of the Year, 1610

Amongst the Irish, many men pass water sitting down, and many women do it standing up. Many people in the country are hideously formed in limbs and body, for in their limbs they lack Nature's good offices. Hence, nowhere are there any people more fairly formed than those in Ireland who are well proportioned, and nowhere are there any worse formed than those who are ill proportioned. So, fittingly, Nature, injured and defiled by their wicked way of life, brings forth such foul, ill-shapen louts from those who sully her so wickedly with illicit intercourse, vile customs, and evil ways.

In Ireland, as in Wales, old women and beldams were accustomed (and still are, according to frequent accounts) to transform themselves often into the likenesses of hares, in order to milk their neighbours' cattle and steal their milk. Often greyhounds run after them in pursuit, thinking that they are hares. Also, some produce fat pink pigs for sale at markets and fairs by their magic arts, but as soon as these pigs cross any water they turn back into their true kind, be it straw, hay, grass, or turf. Such pigs cannot be retained in their swinish form by any art whatsoever beyond the space of three days. Note, what with all these and other marvels and wonders, that new ones often occur at the outermost limits of the world, as if Nature were amusing herself in private with greater licence in the most distant regions than in public near to the centre of the world; it is for this reason that there are many awesome marvels and wonders in Ireland.

Chapter Twenty-Eight

THE MARVELS AND WONDERS OF IRELAND

 any people say that the Island of Life is in the northern region of Ireland; there no one can die, but when its inhabitants are old and troubled by great sickness they are carried out into the neighbouring region to die there. There is another island in Ireland in which no woman can give birth to a child, although she may conceive. There is also an island in which no dead body can rot. In Ultonia, or Ulster, there is an island in a lake which is marvellously divided in two; in one half there is great uproar and disruption caused by devils, and in the other there is great delight and comfort imparted by holy angels. There is also Saint Patrick's Purgatory, which was manifested to him in answer to his prayers for strength when he instructed and preached to unbelievers about the sorrow and pains which evil men are to suffer for their wicked deeds, and about the joy and bliss which good men are to receive for their virtuous deeds. He says that if anyone suffers the pains of that Purgatory, if it is imposed upon him as a penance, he will never suffer the pains of Hell, unless he should finally die without repenting his sins, as will be more fully illustrated at the end of this chapter. But here John Trevisa objects that truly no one can be saved unless he is truly repentant, no matter what penance he may perform; and everyone who is truly repentant at the end of his life shall be saved, even if he has never heard of Saint Patrick's Purgatory.

There is an island in the lake of Connaught, blessed by Saint Brendan. It has no mice, and dead bodies are not buried there, but are kept above ground and do not rot. In Mamonia or Munster there is a well; anyone washing himself with its water will grow grey-haired. There is another well in Ultonia or Ulster; anyone who washes in it will never subsequently grow grey-haired. There is a second well in Munster; if anyone touches it, heavy rain will immediately fall in the whole province, never ceasing until a priest who is a pure virgin sings mass in a chapel close by and blesses the water, and sprinkles the well with the milk of a cow of a single colour, thus stilling the well in this strange manner. At Glendalough around the oratory of Saint Kevin,[1] willows bear apples that are more nutritious than tasty, just as if they were fruit-trees; that holy saint caused those apples to be produced by his prayers, in order to cure his sick servant-boy.

There is a lake in Ulster thirty miles long and fifteen miles wide, containing an abundance of fish, out of which the River Bann runs into the

St Kevin's Church with its adjacent round tower at Glendalough, Co. Wicklow – where it is said willows bear apples

northern region of Ocean, the sea surrounding the earth. It is said that the lake began in the following manner: there were people in that region who followed a wicked way of life, copulating with animals; and there was a well in the same region, venerated since time immemorial, which was always kept covered, for if it were left uncovered it would rise and flood the entire country. It so happened that a woman went to the well to fetch water and, leaving the well uncovered, hastened back quickly to her child which was crying in its cradle. Then the well rose so fast that it drowned the woman and her child, transforming the whole region into a lake and a fishpond. There is powerful proof of the truth of this, in that when the weather is clear, men fishing in the lake can see under the water, on the bottom, tall round towers shaped like the steeples and churches of that country.

In the north of Ireland in Ossory, every seventh year, because of the prayer of a holy abbot, a married couple must perforce be exiled and transformed into the form of wolves, and remain so for seven years. Then, if they survive, they return home and resume their own shape, and then another pair has to go forth in their place and be transformed for the next seven years. In this country there is a special lake: if a wooden pole is placed in it, that part of the shaft or pole which is stuck in the bottom will be turned into iron, that part which is in the water will be turned to stone, and that part which remains above the water will retain its true nature as wood. There is also a lake which transforms hazel-wood into ash, and ash into hazel, if it is placed in it. In Ireland there are, in addition, three salmon leaps, where salmon leap upwards over the rocks to the height of a long spear. In Leinster there is also a pond where Saint Colman's[2] birds are to be found; they are called teals, and will come tamely to men's hands. However, if anyone harms them, they fly away and do not return, and the water will grow bitter and stink, and the wrongdoer will not escape without punishment and misfortune unless he make amends.

Ranulph adds that, as far as Saint Patrick's Purgatory is concerned, you are to understand that it refers to the *second* Saint Patrick, who was an abbot, not a bishop. He laboured and endeavoured, whilst he was preaching in Ireland, to turn away those wicked men, who were living like beasts, from

The church of Reglis or Regles, with a map of St Patrick's Purgatory, from James Ware's De Hibernica *(1654)*

their evil way of life, for fear of the pains of Hell, and to strengthen them in virtuous living; but they said they would not be converted unless some of them might know something about the great pains and the great joys that he spoke of. Then Saint Patrick prayed to Almighty God for that, and Our Lord Jesus Christ appeared to Saint Patrick and gave him a staff and led him into a wild place; there He showed him a round pit, dark within, and said that if a man were truly repentant and firm in his faith, he could go down into this pit and walk there for a day and a night, and would see the sorrows and pains of evil men and the joy and bliss of good men. Then Christ vanished from Saint Patrick's sight, and the Saint erected a church there. He placed canons regular[3] in it, and enclosed the pit with a wall which is now at the east end of the church in the churchyard; it is shut fast with a strong door, for no one should foolishly go in without the leave of the bishop or prior of the place. Many men went in and came out again in Saint Patrick's time, telling of the pains and joys they had seen, and the marvels which they saw are still recorded in writing there, for many people amongst them were converted to true faith. But there were also many men who went and never returned. In the time of King Stephen[4] of England, a knight called Owen entered Saint Patrick's Purgatory and returned, remaining for the rest of his life occupied as a monk in the Cistercian abbey of Ludense; he told of many marvels which he had seen in Saint Patrick's Purgatory. The place is called Patrick's Purgatory and the church is called Reglis. No one is instructed to go into that Purgatory, but rather, people are advised that they should not enter it, taking upon themselves an alternative penance. If, however, a man has made a vow and is determined, desiring of necessity to enter it, he must first go to the bishop and then be sent with letters to the prior of the place, and they must both advise him to desist. If he is determined to enter he must spend fifteen days in prayer and fasting, and after that time he must take the Sacrament and be led to the door of the Purgatory in a procession singing the Litany. Yet again he must be advised to abandon his purpose, but if he is steadfast and wishes to enter, the door is to be opened and he is to be blessed and must depart on his way in God's name, and the door is to be shut fast until the following day. At the appropriate time the prior is to come and open the door, and if the man is there he is to lead him into the church with a procession, and there he must remain for fifteen days in prayer and fasting.

Chapter Twenty-Nine

THE MIRACLES OF IRISH SAINTS

ere, Gerald of Wales notes: just as the people of Ireland are more irascible than other nations, and more hasty in obtaining vengeance in their lifetime, so the saints and holy men of this country are more vengeful than the saints of other countries. The clergy of Ireland are chaste and say many prayers and live in great abstinence by day. However, they drink all night, so it is considered a miracle that lechery does not hold sway there, as wine does. The wicked amongst the Irish are the very lowest of the low; just as the virtuous

The rock of Cashel, Co. Tipperary. Site of the Kings of Munster until the twelfth century and then cathedral of the diocese of Cashel

men amongst them are the best of the best, although there may only be a few of them.

The Irish prelates are slow to correct sins, being occupied with contemplation and not with the preaching of God's word. It is for this reason that all the saints of Ireland are confessors, with no martyrs amongst them; something that is hardly surprising, since all the prelates of this country are elected from abbeys to join the clerical leadership, and observe the proper monastic way of life. They are unfamiliar with the duties of clergymen and prelates; therefore, when the Bishop of Cashel was asked how it might be that there were so many saints in Ireland, yet never a martyr amongst their whole number, given that the people are so wicked and irascible and the prelates so careless and slow in correcting sin, he replied very perversely, saying: 'Our people are wicked and irascible enough amongst themselves, but they never lay a hand on God's servants, rather offering them great reverence and respect; but Englishmen, who know how to make martyrs and were accustomed to practise that art are coming into this country.' Ranulph explains that the bishop said this because King Henry the Second had just recently come into Ireland after causing the martyrdom of Saint Thomas of Canterbury.

Gerald of Wales relates that in Ireland, Wales, and Scotland there are bells, staffs with curved heads, and other such objects which are held in great veneration and honour as relics, so that the people of that country dread swearing on any of these bells and curved staffs more than on the Gospel. The chief of all those relics is considered to be Jesus's staff at Dublin; they say that the first Saint Patrick drove the snakes out of Ireland with it. Saint Augustine,[1] in *The City of God*, observes that, if people ask how it can happen that different kinds and species of animals, begotten by natural breeding between males and females, come to inhabit islands after Noah's Flood, it is generally held that such animals swam from one island to the next, or else that men, sailing to islands, brought such animals with them for the sake of hunting, or else that angels at Almighty God's command put them onto islands, or alternatively that the earth first brought them forth, fulfilling God's commandment to the earth to bring forth grass and living creatures.

St Patrick's bell, with its shrine. Such bells were much venerated amongst the Irish; they dreaded swearing on them

EPILOGUE

Here ends *The Description of Britain*, containing England, Wales, and Scotland; because Ireland is under English rule and has remained so for a very long time I have added its description to that of Britain. I have taken the whole from the *Polychronicon* of Ranulph Higden. Because it is necessary for all Englishmen to know the special nature, endowments, and marvels of these countries, I have printed them, following the translation of John Trevisa, who at Lord Berkeley's request translated the entire *Polychronicon* into English. This was finished by me, William Caxton, on the eighteenth day of August in the year of Our Lord God 1480, in the twentieth year of the reign of King Edward the Fourth.

NOTES

INTRODUCTION

1   See ch.29 n.1.

2   The early fifth-century historian. Saint Augustine sent him to Palestine to ask for Saint Jerome's support in combating the Pelagian heresy. He wrote an *Historia adversus paganos* to refute pagan arguments that Rome had fallen on bad times because she had abandoned the classical gods in favour of Christianity.

3   See ch.1 n.4.

4   The famous Northumbrian scholar-monk and historian, *c*. AD 673–735. His most famous work is the *Ecclesiastical History*, completed *c*. AD 731.

5   See ch.1 n.6.

6   Monk and historian, *c*. AD 1090–*c*. 1143. He wrote a secular history of England, the *Gesta Regum Anglorum* (1120); and a religious history of England, the *Gesta Pontificum Anglorum* (1125).

7   Lived *c*. AD 1100–154 AD. His *History of the Kings of Britain* (trs. Lewis Thorpe, Penguin 1966) is of more legendary than historical value.

8   Or Gerald de Barri, *c*. AD 1147–1223, the historian and topographer. His *Description of Wales* exists in a modern English translation by Lewis Thorpe (Penguin, 1978) and his *History and Topography of Ireland* in a translation by John J. O'Meara (Penguin, 1982).

CHAPTER ONE

1   All that Geoffrey of Monmouth says in *The History of the Kings of Britain* (henceforward *HKB*) i 16 is that the island was called Albion. He does not provide an etymology. The Emperor Diocletian ruled in the Eastern Roman Empire AD 284–305. Lactantius, *De mortibus persecutorum* VII, mentions that he had an unnamed daughter, but there is no mention of thirty-two sisters or of any connection with the British Isles.

2   Geoffrey of Monmouth, *HKB* i 3, tells of the birth of Brutus, great-grandson of the famous Aeneas who escaped from Troy to found the kingdom of Italy. Prophecies that he would cause the death of his parents, wander in exile through many lands, and rise to the highest honour, were all fulfilled. *HKB* i 15 and i 16 tell how he landed at Totnes and settled in Britain (then Albion).

3   Bede, *Ecclesiastical History* (henceforward *EH*) i 15 tells of the coming of 'the Angles, or Saxons' at the invitation of King Vortigern. However, later in the same chapter he distinguishes between the three Germanic tribes to invade and settle in Britain: the Angles, Saxons, and Jutes. Modern scholarship is less sure than Bede of the patterns of invasion by the Germanic tribes.

4   Isidore of Seville lived *c*. 560–636 and was Archbishop of Seville from *c*. AD 600. His *Etymologies* are an encyclopaedic work full of contemporary secular and religious knowledge, much of it presented by way of fanciful etymologies of the words which formed the headings of the subjects treated. In the case of 'Anglia' the etymology is more on course than usual.

5   For Bede's explanation see *EH* ii 1.

6   Twelfth-century author of a History of Britain.

7   The famous King of the Franks who lived *c*. AD 742–814. From 800 he was the first Emperor of the Holy Roman Empire.

CHAPTER TWO

1   The Morini are possibly the Flemings (see J.S.P. Tatlock, *The Legendary History of Britain: Geoffrey of Monmouth's Historia Regum Britanniae and its Early Vernacular Versions* (U. of California Press, 1950) pp. 93-94.) Gessorico is unidentified.

2   Pliny the Elder (AD 23/24–79), author of the *Natural History*, a lengthy encyclopaedic work.

3   The so-called island between the junction of the Bahr-el-Abiad with the true Nile and that of the Atbara with the Nile. The city of Meroe, known to the Greek historian Herodotus, was the capital of the kingdom of Napata.

4   A land to the far north, reputedly six days' sailing north of Britain, first described by the Greek navigator Pytheas (*c*. 310–306 BC). It is uncertain whether he meant Iceland or Norway. Beyond it lay the frozen sea, and it was regarded as the northernmost part of the inhabited world. Procopius, the sixth-century Greek historian, called it an 'island' and gave Scandinavia the name of Thule.

5   The Spaniard Paulus Orosius, a pupil of Saint Augustine of Hippo in the early fifth century and author of a world history from the Christian viewpoint, the *Historia adversus paganos*.

6   Author, fl. shortly after AD 200, of a geographical summary of knowledge about the world, containing information about the customs, produce, origins and history of the various countries. It is heavily dependent upon Pliny's *Natural History*.

CHAPTER THREE

1   Unidentified.

2   Samos is an island off western Asia Minor, traditionally noted for many trades and products, though not particularly pottery; nonetheless the Roman writers Plautus, Martial and Pliny used its name to refer to a common and inexpensive type of tableware. Caxton and his sources are using the allusion to suggest richness in all types of ceramic productions.

3   The medieval County of Flanders, situated approximately opposite the projection of Kent, was bounded to the east by the County of Artois and to the west by the Duchy of Brabant.

4   The medieval County of Holland was much smaller than the modern country, extending from the tip of the Hook of Holland down to the Duchy of Brabant.

5   The far south-western area of what is now modern France.

6   Possibly tin.

7   The Roman Emperor Octavian became a favourite figure in medieval romances about Charlemagne. A Middle English romance about him is extant.

CHAPTER FOUR

1   The Roman goddess equated with the Greek Athena, virgin goddess of wisdom. She had a particular connection with water; hence at Bath, for example, she was identified with the local water-deity Sul.

2 Probably High Peak in the Derbyshire Peak District.

3 Unidentified.

4 (i) Saint Audrey, or Aethelthryth, or Etheldreda (b. *c.* AD 630, d. 679), was the daughter of King Anna of the East Angles. Though twice married, she is celebrated liturgically as a virgin, having refused marital relations with her second husband (and probably her first too), who set her free to become a nun. She founded and was abbess of a double monastery at Ely, which became a centre of pilgrimage to her shrine after her death; (ii) King Edmund (b. AD 841, d. 869) of East Anglia was killed by invading Danes, and quickly became revered as a martyr. His body was enshrined at Bury St Edmunds; (iii) Alphege or Aelfheah (b. AD 954, d. 1012, Archbishop of Canterbury, was killed by drunken Danes who had taken him prisoner. He was venerated as a martyr; (iv) Edgar, King of Wessex AD 959–75, though never a saint, was held in great honour for his patronage of later tenth-century ecclesiastical reform; (v) Cuthbert (b. *c.* AD 634, d. 687, a Northumbrian, became a monk, for some time a solitary, and finally Bishop of Lindisfarne. His remains were eventually translated to Durham Cathedral; (vi) Edward could be either King Edward the Martyr (b. *c.* AD 962, d. 978, son of King Edgar of Wessex (see (iv) above, murdered (not martyred) for political reasons, or King Edward the Confessor (b. *c.* AD 1004, d. 1066), noted for his piety. Edward the Martyr's body was translated to the nunnery church of Shaftesbury; Edward the Confessor was buried in the church of the abbey at Westminster, and his remains were translated to a place behind the high altar in AD 1268. They still remain there in their medieval shrine.

CHAPTER FIVE

1 It is not possible to equate this, or many others amongst the place-names mentioned, with known modern locations.

2 See Geoffrey of Monmouth, *HKB* ii 1.

3 The famous King of Mercia who ruled AD 757–796. The huge earthwork attributed to him by both English and Welsh tradition defined the boundary between his territory and that of the Welsh.

CHAPTER SIX

1 See Bede, *EH* i. 3. Claudius was Roman Emperor AD 41–54, and Vespasian eventually succeeded to power AD 69–79.

2 The Latin poet who lived 70–19 BC, author of *The Aeneid* and *The Georgics*.

3 Scylla, originally a six-headed sea-monster, ever ready to devour mariners, and living opposite Charybdis, a whirlpool. She was often rationalized into a rock or other dangerous natural feature.

4 Saint Augustine of Canterbury, formerly prior of a monastery in Rome, was sent by Pope Gregory the Great to convert the English in AD 596–7.

CHAPTER SEVEN

1 The form of this name varies greatly. In Geoffrey of Monmouth, *HKB* ii 17, and in Ranulph Higden i 50, it appears as 'Molmutius', in John Trevisa's Middle English translation of Higden as 'Moliuntius', and in an anonymous fifteenth-century translation as 'Molimicius'. Words containing a predominance of letters formed by minim-strokes are particularly vulnerable to such transformations.

CHAPTER EIGHT

1 See Geoffrey of Monmouth, *HKB* ii. 4. King Locrinus loved Estrild, the daughter of the King of Germany, and could not forget her even when he married another woman, Gwendolen. He later deserted her for Estrild, who had meanwhile borne him an extraordinarily beautiful daughter, Habren. Gwendolen took her revenge by waging a fatal war on Locrinus

and by drowning Estrild and Habren in the River Severn, which she ordered to be named after Habren.

CHAPTER NINE

1 On the mysterious begetting of the enchanter and seer Merlin, and on his coming to public notice in 'Kaermerdin', see Geoffrey of Monmouth, *HKB* vi 17 and 18.

2 The identity of Achamannus is uncertain. The former name for Bath given by Geoffrey of Monmouth, *HKB* ii 10, is 'Kaerbadum'.

3 See Geoffrey of Monmouth, *HKB* iii 20, for his fame as a town-planner and for the naming of the city which later became London after him.

4 A monk, and the earliest British historian (*c.* AD 500–70) His *De Excidio et Conquestu Britanniae* covers the history of the Celts from the coming of the Romans to his own day.

5 The Roman Emperor who invaded Britain in 55 and 54 BC.

6 Hadrian's Wall, erected in AD 122–6, stretching from Wallsend-on-Tyne to Bowness-on-Solway, was restored by the Emperor Septimius Severus in AD 205–207.

7 See Geoffrey of Monmouth, *HKB* iii 16 and 17 for the story of Elidurus and Archgalon/Archgallo.

8 See Geoffrey of Monmouth, *HKB* iv 16 and 17, on Arvira(r)gus, a valiant British king who fought against Vespasian, and his equally brave son Marius, whose victory over the Picts was commemorated by an inscribed stone.

9 According to Geoffrey of Monmouth, *HKB* iv 15, Genuissa was the daughter of the Roman Emperor Claudius and was given in marriage to the British king, Arviragus (see n. 8 above).

10 Martyred Romano-Britons, reputedly put to death at Caerleon, possibly in the middle of the third century AD.

11 Saint Alban, martyred at Verulamium (now St Albans) *c.* AD 209, was a Romano-British Christian. He was put to death for sheltering a Christian on the run during the persecution instigated by the Emperor Diocletian. In some versions, including Geoffrey of Monmouth's (*HKB* v 5), the refugee is named as Alban's confessor Amphibalus.

12 Gerald of Wales says that the Emperor Henry V died as a hermit near Chester, adding that he lived for ten years there under the name of 'Godescalle'.

13 According to Gerald of Wales, Harold II fled, wounded, from the battle of Hastings, to Chester, where he lived on as an anchorite in the chapel of Saint James, close to Saint John's church.

CHAPTER TEN

1 A triple division of England, based on the different prevailing legal customs in each, grew up in Anglo-Saxon England. The Danelaw, which had come under strong Scandinavian influence as the result of Danish invasions, covered northern and north-eastern England, the East Midlands and East Anglia, and the northern Home Counties.

2 A fief is a landed estate held by service to a superior lord.

CHAPTER ELEVEN

1 See Geoffrey of Monmouth, *HKB* iii 13, for the model British ruler Guitelinus and his wise and skilled wife who reputedly devised the *Lex Martiana*.

2 Alfred the Great of Wessex, who ruled from AD 871–99.

3 Burglary, or breaking and entering.

4 Asylum or sanctuary.

CHAPTER TWELVE

1 The Roman Emperor Septimius Severus ruled AD 193–211.

2 Harold II, King of England for nine months in AD 1066. He died at the Battle of Hastings, fighting against William ('the Conqueror') of Normandy.

3 Dionysius Exiguus, a monk in Rome *c.* AD 500.

4 Baldred was deposed and driven out of Kent in AD 825.

5 Ruled Kent in the last quarter of the fifth century.

CHAPTER THIRTEEN

1 A circular band of white woollen material with two hanging strips, marked with six purple crosses. It is worn on the shoulders by the Pope and granted by him to archbishops.

2 i.e. during the sixth century AD.

3 Archbishop of Canterbury AD 667–90.

4 Thought to have reigned in Wessex AD 611–43.

5 King of Wessex from the mid-seventh century to AD 672.

6 Leutherius or Leuthere was the nephew of Agilbert, Bishop of the West Saxons. Leutherius was consecrated Bishop of Winchester in AD 670.

7 The son of Alfred the Great, he reigned in Wessex from AD 889–924.

8 King of England AD 1087–1100.

9 King of England AD 1100–35.

10 King of Wessex AD 973–5.

11 Bishop of York AD 625 until his flight from the heathen King Cadwallon in AD 632.

12 King of Northumbria AD 633–41. He died fighting against the heathen King Penda of Mercia.

13 The reference is to the dissension between the followers of Celtic Christianity, which had been brought to Northumbria by Saint Aidan during King Oswald's reign, and those of Roman Christianity, brought to Northumbria by Paulinus during King Edwin's reign. The factions differed in their liturgy, ritual, organization, the form of tonsure adopted, and their method of calculating the date of Easter.

14 See ch. 4, n.4.

15 The Lionheart', who ruled AD 1189–99.

16 Probably Henry III, who died in 1272 and was therefore the most recent Henry to whom Ranulph Higden's Latin, on which both John Trevisa and Caxton depend, could be referring.

CHAPTER FOURTEEN

1 They originally inhabited Ireland. Their migration to Scotland is described later in the chapter.

2 Inhabitants of Flanders, on which see ch.3, n.3. The early Flemish settlement in West Wales took place during the reign of Henry I, AD 1100–35.

CHAPTER FIFTEEN

1 Son of the Dane Cnut, or Canute, whom he failed to succeed to the English throne in 1035, because he could not immediately leave his inheritance in Denmark. In 1040 he landed in England with his troops and assumed power until his early death in 1042 'as he stood at his drink' at a wedding feast.

2 The possible candidates are Pope Eugenius I (Pope 655–7), Pope Eugenius II (Pope 824–7), and Pope Eugenius III (Pope 1145–53). I have been unable to trace the comment.

3 There are numerous references to Argus, Tantalus and Daedalus amongst classical authors. For Sardanapalus see John Gower, *Confessio Amantis*, ed. G.C. Macaulay (Early English Texts Society, 1900), vol. II, bk. vii, ll. 4313–43.

4 Unidentified.

CHAPTER SIXTEEN

1 The King of Troy at the time of its destruction. For the tradition that the British were descended from refugee Trojan stock, see Geoffrey of Monmouth, *HKB* iv 1.

CHAPTER SEVENTEEN

1 See Geoffrey of Monmouth, *HKB* ii 7 and 8. He was the father of twenty sons and thirty daughters, including Gwalaes.

CHAPTER NINETEEN

1 The exact dates of the satirist's life are not known. He was probably born between AD 50 and 65, and was still writing in AD 127.

CHAPTER TWENTY-ONE

1 Saint Chad or Ceadda, educated by Saint Aidan at Lindisfarne; a notably humble man who ended his days in AD 672 as Bishop of Lichfield.

2 *c.* AD 628–704, who in 679 became the ninth abbot of Iona. He was instrumental in promoting the Roman rather than the Celtic method of calculating the date of Easter.

3 Constantine the Great, *c.* AD 285–337, the Roman Emperor famous for his conversion to Christianity.

4 The Eastern Roman Emperor Theodosius II, ruling AD 408–50.

CHAPTER TWENTY-THREE

1 For Hiberus and his brother Hermon see Gerald of Wales, *The History and Topography of Ireland* (henceforward *HTI*), trs. John J. O'Meara (Penguin, 1982), ch. 90.

CHAPTER TWENTY-SIX

1 See Gerald of Wales, *HTI*, ch. 90.

2 On Gaitelus or Gaidelus, nephew of Phenius, see Gerald of Wales, *HTI*, ch. 91.

3 On Fedlimidius or Feidhlimidh, see Gerald of Wales, *HTI*, ch. 110. He lived in the second quarter of the ninth century.

4 On Gurmundus see Gerald of Wales, *HTI*, chs. 112-114.

CHAPTER TWENTY-SEVEN

1 These technical details of the musical skills of the Irish are taken from Gerald of Wales, *HTI*, ch. 94.

2 The medieval church regarded as very special the spiritual relationships between godchildren and godparents. At Christian baptism, they are witnesses who assume responsibility for the spiritual upbringing of the newly-baptized, and who make promises of renunciation, faith and obedience on behalf of infant candidates.

CHAPTER TWENTY-EIGHT

1 Or Coemgen, an Irish abbot, d. 618 AD. His association with the world of nature is particularly marked in the many medieval stories attached to his name.

2 Colman is such a common name amongst Irish saints that it is impossible to be sure which one is being referred to.

3 The term 'canon', originally applied to all clergy on the official staff of a diocese, became narrowed in meaning to secular clergy attached to a cathedral or collegiate church. They are 'regular' because they follow a religious Rule (in Latin, *regula*).

4 Reigned AD 1135–54.

CHAPTER TWENTY-NINE

1 Augustine of Hippo, AD 354–430, bishop and doctor of the church and author of many sermons and treatises, including *On Christian Doctrine*, *The City of God* (referred to here) and his *Confessions*. He is to be distinguished from the Saint Augustine who arrived in England in AD 597 on a papal mission to convert the English to Christianity.

INDEX

Note: Page numbers in italics indicate illustrations

ACKNOWLEDGMENTS

I am very grateful to many friends and colleagues for advice and help, in particular Brenda Bolton, Mary Anne Macdonald, Lucinda Rumsey and Peter Denley. Above all I am grateful to Deborah Pownall, whose painstaking picture research has taught me a great deal and given much enjoyment.

Photographs and illustrations were supplied or are reproduced by kind permission of the following:

Black and white Aerofilms, 48, 55; BBC Hulton Picture Library, 105, 150; Bodleian Library, 100; Janet and Colin Bord, 52, 85, 141; British Library, 34, 36, 49, 64, 88, 97, 108, 116, 119, 136, 137, 160; J. Allan Cash, 33 (bottom), 41, 45, 57, 69; Conway Library, Courtauld Institute of Art, 155; Fortean Picture Library, 52; Sonia Halliday, 120/21; Robert Harding, 38, 144, 145; Michael Holford, 80 (left); Ministry of Public Buildings and Works, 145; National Monuments Record, 125; National Museum of Ireland, 169; National Museum of Wales, 128; Nottingham Central Library, 65; Public Records Office, 129; Ronald Sheridan, 76, 80 (right), 117, 132, 153; Weidenfeld and Nicolson, 37, 44, 81, 152, 156.

Colour Aberystwyth Central Library, 130; Ashmolean Museum, 79; Janet and Colin Bord, 146, 163, 167; Bridgeman Art Library, 31, 115; British Library, 35, 39 (bottom), 47 (bottom), 58, 62, 63, 86, 98, 103, 122/3, 151; 'Britain on View', BTA, 51; J. Allan Cash, 42/3, 91, 126, 127, 135, 138/9, 147; E.T. Archive, 59; Sonia Halliday, 39 (top), 83, 95, 110, 131; Robert Harding, 66, 67, 70/71, 99; Michael Holford, 47 (top), 82, 90, 106/7; A.F. Kersting, 94; Ronald Sheridan, 30; Trinity College Library, 159.